FANNY CROSBY

THE HYMN WRITER

BERNARD RUFFIN

BARBOUR
PUBLISHING

© 1976 by the Pilgrim Press

Print ISBN 978-1-62416-125-4

eBook Editions:
Adobe Digital Edition (.epub) 978-1-62416-427-9
Kindle and MobiPocket Edition (.prc) 978-1-62416-426-2

All scripture quotations, unless otherwise noted, are taken from the King James Version of the Bible.

Cover illustration: Greg Copeland
Cover design: Kirk DouPonce

Published by Barbour Publishing, Inc., P.O. Box 719, Uhrichsville, Ohio 44683, www.barbourbooks.com

Our mission is to publish and distribute inspirational products offering exceptional value and biblical encouragement to the masses.

Member of the
Evangelical Christian
Publishers Association

Printed in the United States of America.

CONTENTS

1
ALMOST A SAINT

The year is 1910. The place is Perth Amboy, New Jersey. A cab driver stops his horses to pick up two passengers: a middle-aged clergyman and a withered old woman, apparently blind, ravaged, and wasted almost beyond belief, bent nearly double with age. But as the coach jolts along to the railroad depot, the hackman becomes aware of something unusual about this ancient woman. She speaks to the clergyman in a voice not dry and quavering, but clear and high, mellow and young. Far from senile, the lady's mind is as fresh and young as her voice. She evidently is a woman of great intellect and refinement. She and the clergyman are discussing some point of theology. The coachman, paying more attention to what she is saying than to the road, listens intently to the wit and wisdom of the elderly lady.

"This is Fanny Crosby, the hymn writer," the minister informs him.

The hackman is stunned. He takes off his hat and weeps openly. At the depot, he hails a policeman. "This is Miss Fanny Crosby, who wrote 'Safe in the Arms of Jesus.' I want you to help this young man get her safely to the train."

The policeman, too, is stunned. "I sure will!" Falteringly, he adds to the woman, "We sang your hymn 'Safe in the Arms of Jesus' last week, at my little girl's funeral."

He looks at the ground with reddened, shining eyes. "Aunt Fanny" takes his enormous arm in her skinny hands and says, with great feeling and tenderness, "My boy, I call all policemen and railroad men 'my boys'; they take such good care of me wherever I go. God bless your dear heart! You shall have my prayers. And tell your dear wife that your dear little girl is 'safe in the arms of Jesus.' "

The constable weeps openly.

Who was Fanny Crosby, this strange little woman dressed in the style of seventy years before, with the green glasses and the crucifix on her breast? Who was this blind woman whose name was so revered by people on the street?

Today, she often is remembered as the author of mawkish Victorian hymns, trite and hackneyed. Among many liberal-minded clergy, her name is a byword for bad church music and bad theology; she seems to them to have been a neurotic woman of syrupy literary bent.

And that's if she's remembered at all. For most people, the name Fanny Crosby conjures up an absolute blank.

Was she indeed simply a third-rate hack poet whose fame justly faded generations ago? Or was she more than we realize today, someone whose life story is worth retelling? Did she make a significant contribution to American society, or was she overrated in her day?

How different was the place of Fanny Crosby in the estimation of our forebears! Far from being the epitome of a bad hymn writer, Fanny Crosby in her day was considered the greatest in America. Johann Strauss reigned as the waltz king in Vienna and John

Philip Sousa the march king in Washington; Fanny Crosby reigned as the hymn queen in New York during the latter nineteenth and early twentieth centu-

> **FANNY CROSBY REIGNED AS THE HYMN QUEEN DURING THE LATTER NINETEENTH AND EARLY TWENTIETH CENTURIES.**

ries. Charles H. Gabriel (1856–1932), himself a noted hymn writer and author of several popu-lar songs, at her death la-mented the loss of the woman whose "name, suspended as a halo above modern hymnology. . .will live on as long as people sing the Gospel." William Alfred Quayle (1860–1925), a Methodist bishop, poet, and theologian, called her the "modern Saint Ce-celia." George Coles Stebbins (1846–1945), a prominent hymn writer and evangelical singer, attributed all his success as a hymn tune composer to the poetry of the men and women who supplied him with verse, especially to his beloved "Aunt Fanny." He wrote in 1905, "The most distinguishing thing about my life has been my friends, Fanny Crosby, and Moody and Sankey. . . . They have made me what I am."

In his 1924 autobiography, Stebbins wrote, "There was prob-ably no writer in her day who appealed more to the valid experi-ence of the Christian life or who expressed more sympathetically the deep longings of the human heart than Fanny Crosby." In 1904, the well-known singing evangelist, Ira D. Sankey, partner and colleague of D. L. Moody, said the success of their evangelical campaigns resulted largely from Fanny Crosby's hymns.

During the era (1870–1920) of the "gospel song," a light, infor-mal hymn written in the style of the popular ballad, Fanny Crosby reigned supreme. Her hymns were sung all over the world. During an evangelical campaign in the British Isles, Sankey took a short vacation to the Swiss Alps, where he was astounded to hear peasants singing, beneath the window of his inn, Fanny Crosby's "Pass Me Not, O Gentle Saviour" in German. That hymn was said to have been a favorite of Queen Victoria and the Prince and Princess of Wales. "Safe in the Arms of Jesus" was played by a brass band at the funeral of President Grant in 1885 and, the same year, was sung at the funeral of Lord Shaftsbury, a founder of the YMCA. During the early 1900s, an American clergyman traveling through the Arabian desert was amazed to hear Bedouins in their tents singing "Saved by Grace," presumably in Arabic.

But Fanny was known for more than her hymns. She was one of the three most prominent figures in American evangelical religious life in the last quarter of the nineteenth century (Moody and Sankey were the others). She was famous as a preacher and lecturer and was a devoted home-mission worker. Many times when she spoke at a church, people would be lined up for at least a block before the service began.

SHE WAS CALLED "THE PROTESTANT SAINT."

She was venerated as practically a living saint in her later years; in fact, she was called "the Protestant saint" or "the Methodist saint." When she was at home, she was a virtual "prisoner of the confessional" for the scores of people who came from all over the world to seek her advice and prayers.

In her ninety-five years, Fanny Crosby wrote approximately nine thousand hymns—more than anyone else in recorded Christian history—and more than a thousand secular poems. She was noted for her concerts on harp and organ. To our grandparents and great-grandparents, she was revered.

The popular congregational and Sunday school hymn originated with her generation of hymn writers, of whom she was the chief example. Before then, many hymns were staid, formal, and rather cold. Fanny and her colleagues worked to develop a kind of hymn, in the popular idiom, that appealed to the emotions of the worshipper. In this sense, she can be considered the grandmother of latter-day pop hymns and praise songs. In fact, she may be regarded as the grandmother of all hymns that address the personal feelings and emotions of the singers, all hymns written in the popular vein.

This is the story of a woman of humble origins, blind almost from birth, who achieved fame as a poet, educator, and musician before becoming known throughout the English-speaking world as a hymn writer and, finally, almost as a saint.

2
BLINDED

Southeast, New York, in Putnam County, was more a geographical district than a town in 1820. It was a rural area of forest and farmland, with a few tiny hamlets here and there. The largest village was Doanesburg, then a thriving center with a Presbyterian church, a parsonage, a post office, a school, and even a library.

The countryside round about was dotted with trees and marked with the stone walls typical of New England. The soil was not good, producing more rocks than crops, and it was virtually impossible for a small farmer to survive. Many men either hired themselves out as hands on the estates of one of the several great landowners or combined with fathers, brothers, or cousins to farm jointly a substantial tract of land. Most of the more than nineteen hundred inhabitants of Southeast in 1820 were "peasants." In those days, the term did not have the lowly meaning it has today; it simply denoted rural working folk. Fanny Crosby often spoke in later years of the "humble peasants" from which she sprang.

Almost everyone in Southeast was of solid Yankee stock, descendants of original settlers of the Massachusetts Bay Colony

> FANNY CROSBY OFTEN SPOKE OF THE "HUMBLE PEASANTS" FROM WHICH SHE SPRANG.

and of largely English extraction. Familially, the area was comprised of clans, and in 1820, virtually everyone seemed to have been related to one another. There were only a few dozen family names in the area, and certain families were very large. The largest of the Southeast clans was the Crosby family, numbering eleven households. Sometimes the various families who comprised a clan would be clustered in a settlement bearing their name. The community where Fanny Crosby was born was named for the Gay clan, who lived there in large numbers.

The men wore black clothing, and most sported long, full beards. The women, too, wore black, and their full-skirted "Basque dresses" with stiff, white collars and cuffs had buttons all the way down the front, from neck to hip.

They were pious folk, these Southeast peasants. The Presbyterian church still taught almost unadulterated Puritan-Calvinist doctrine, with its tenets of "irresistible grace," "double predestination," and the need for a distinct personal conversion experience.

Although poor, they were literate, managing somehow to sandwich, between long hours of hard labor, a few years at the little red district schoolhouse. There, the children of Southeast would learn from a man or woman who had gone scarcely further than the highest level of training being taught. But they learned! These "humble peasants," few of whom went beyond sixth grade, would read and write poetry as they sat by the fire on winter nights when the work was done. They could recite Milton and Shakespeare and Chapman's *Homer*. All of them knew Bunyan's classic, *The Pilgrim's Progress,* and, of course, the King James translation of the Holy Bible.

A half-hour's walk along a winding road from Doanesburg was the settlement known as Gayville. One of the half-dozen dwellings in that wooded paradise was a small, rough, one-story frame cottage. Situated near the crest of a hill, it looked out onto a landscape of rolling hills dotted with trees. Behind it was an open field surrounded by a virgin forest full of towering oaks and maples, with thick underbrush.

This was the home of Sylvanus Crosby, a veteran of the War of 1812, who was probably in his mid-forties. A poor man eking out a marginal existence through his farm labor, he claimed direct descent from William Brewster, one of the Pilgrim fathers. Arriving on the *Mayflower* in 1620, Brewster had helped establish Plymouth Plantation. Toward the end of the seventeenth century, one of his descendants, Patience Freeman, married Eleazer Crosby.

Eleazer was the grandson of Simon and Ann Crosby, who came from England in 1635 and settled near Boston. Simon Crosby came from an old Yorkshire family. Born in 1608, he married Ann Brigham (1606–1675) and came to the New World. He helped found Harvard College soon after his arrival, and died a few years later. One of his sons, Eleazer's father, Thomas (1634–1702), was graduated from the college his father helped found. Although never ordained, he conducted services as a "religious teacher" on Cape Cod; he also was connected with the shipping business.

Eleazer had a son named Isaac, born in Harwich, near Cape Cod, in 1719. Shortly after that, the family moved to New Milford, Connecticut, and then to Southeast, New York. It is not recorded how long Eleazer lived, but Patience, his wife, lived to be 103 years old and until her early eighties made horseback trips alone to visit relatives at Cape Cod.

Isaac Crosby married a woman named Mercy Foster who bore him nineteen children. The youngest of these was Sylvanus, who was born during the Revolutionary War. Despite his being in his late fifties at its outbreak, Isaac volunteered to serve in the war.

Isaac won no laurels, but he managed to return home alive and to stay that way until he was past one hundred. He and his descendants were proud of his service and of the

"WHEN GENERAL WARREN WAS KILLED AT BUNKER HILL, IT WAS A CROSBY WHO CAUGHT UP THE FLAG."

exploits of other distant relatives during the Revolution. Fanny liked to recall some of the tales she was told as a child. "When General Warren was killed at Bunker Hill," she wrote, "it was a Crosby who caught up the flag as it fell from his hands."

Around 1798, when Sylvanus was about twenty-one years old, he married Eunice Paddock. Sylvanus and Eunice had four children, each six years older than the next. The eldest, born in 1799, was named Mercy, after Sylvanus's mother. She was followed by Theda in 1805, then Joseph in 1811, and finally Mary, whom everyone called Polly, in 1817.

Sylvanus tried to farm the little plot of ground as best he could, scratching out an existence for his family. By 1820 he was not the sole breadwinner, for Mercy had married and lived with her husband in the family cottage.

Mercy's husband, John Crosby, was an older man, perhaps not much younger than Sylvanus. He probably was a cousin (marrying a cousin was not unusual in Southeast). Nothing is known of John Crosby, and since he died when Fanny was a baby, she had no personal recollection of him. She was always told he had been an extremely ambitious, hardworking man who, like Sylvanus, apparently was a veteran of the War of 1812. He had been married before and had one daughter, Laura, who was about the same age as Mercy's sister Theda.

On March 24, 1820, two months before her twenty-first birthday,

Mercy gave birth to a daughter, christened Frances Jane Crosby after one of her mother's numerous aunts, Fannie Paddock Curtis.

By late April, the Crosbys were alarmed. Something was wrong with the baby's eyes. In later years, Fanny spoke of a sickness that made her eyes "very weak." More disconcerting, the family was unable to obtain competent medical assistance; the community doctor was away.

> **THE CROSBYS WERE ALARMED. SOMETHING WAS WRONG WITH THE BABY'S EYES.**

Finally, they found a man who claimed to be a physician. Eighty-six years later, Fanny wrote of him as "a stranger." Whoever he was, he horrified the Crosbys by putting a hot poultice on the baby's inflamed eyes. The "doctor" insisted the extreme heat would not hurt the child's eyes and would draw out the infection. When he had finished his treatments, the infection gradually cleared up, but ugly white scars formed on the eyes. As the months went by, little Fanny Jane made no response when objects were held before her face.

The "doctor" did not remain long in Southeast. The Crosbys accused the man outright of blinding the baby and stirred up such indignation in Gayville, Doanesburg, and neighboring hamlets that the man, no doubt fearing lynching, fled the vicinity and was never heard from again.

Further disaster was to strike the household of Sylvanus Crosby. November 1820 was cold and rainy, but John Crosby labored in the fields, even in the downpours. One night he came in badly chilled. The next day he was seriously ill, and a few days later, he died.

The Crosbys considered themselves devout Puritans, and Mercy, a widow at twenty-one, was comforted in the hope that she and her husband would meet again one day in heaven. But on earth, Mercy realized her father could not support a household of six persons alone. So shortly after her husband's body was lowered into an unmarked grave in the Doanesburg cemetery, she hired herself out as a maidservant for a wealthy family nearby. Fanny Jane would be taken good care of by Mercy's mother.

Though desperately poor, the Crosbys, buoyed by their devout faith, were a happy family. During the day, Grandmother Eunice and her middle daughter, Theda, kept house and cared for Fanny and Polly, who were more like sisters than niece and aunt. Joseph by now was no doubt assisting his father in farm work. In the evenings when Sylvanus, Joseph, and Mercy returned home, the family would sit reading and reciting poetry. As a little girl, Fanny Jane listened with rapt attention to the ballad of "Rinaldo Rhinaldine," the robber chieftain, to the tales of Robin Hood, to the *Iliad* and the *Odyssey*, to John Milton, and to the Bible.

Eunice took a special interest in Fanny, and during the child's first four or five years was closer to her than her mother. "My grandmother was more to me than I can ever express by word or pen," Fanny wrote. When it had become obvious that Fanny Jane was deprived of eyesight, Eunice decided she would be her granddaughter's eyes. She firmly resolved that Fanny Jane would not be a helpless invalid, dependent on others as so many blind people were in those days. She

> EUNICE DECIDED SHE WOULD BE HER GRANDDAUGHTER'S EYES.

undertook to describe the physical world to the child in terms she hoped she would understand. Eighty years later, Fanny remembered her grandmother "taking me on her knee and rocking me while she told me of the beautiful sun with its sunrise and sunset." How Eunice could describe colors to a child blind almost from birth is not so great a mystery, for Fanny Jane could perceive very intense light and sometimes could distinguish various hues. Eunice also taught the blind child about birds:

One day I heard a strange sound coming from the meadow, saying, "Whippoorwill." Grandma told me about the bird which gave out that curious note and described its mottled wings and reddish brown breast, and its bristled mouth, with its white bristled tail.*

How did Fanny understand what "bristled" meant? Eunice would place in her hands a surface similar to the one she was trying to describe. Afterward, whenever Fanny heard the sound of the whippoorwill, she knew the color and shape of the bird that produced that sound. Eunice also taught her about the meadowlark, cuckoo, song sparrow, goldfinch, yellow warbler, wren, and robin.

The remarkable Eunice, a peasant from the remote backwoods of New York, was as skillful and successful in instructing the blind child as many with degrees. She taught her granddaughter about botany. By the time Fanny was three or four, the violet was her favorite flower and would remain so for the rest of her life. In autumn, Eunice took Fanny on walks over the hills, telling her about the trees and their leaves. Fanny Jane came to know the trees as she did the flowers—by means of touch and smell—and the leaves by "handling and remembering." Eunice realized Fanny's memory would have to play an especially important role in her life, so she began exercising it. Eunice

> FANNY CAME TO KNOW THE TREES AS SHE DID THE FLOWERS— BY MEANS OF TOUCH AND SMELL.

would gather up piles of autumn leaves and have Fanny play with them. "Now what tree is *this* one from?" she would ask. It was from the early training at Grandma's hands that she acquired a capacity for detailed description, and it was from this training that she acquired a wonderful memory.

Eunice also had a great influence on Fanny's religious development. All the Crosbys were devout Christians, but Eunice seems to have been practically angelic. Grandma saw all the world as God's book and each natural phenomenon as a manifestation of God. Like many people of her day and of earlier generations, she saw nature as a mirror of the spiritual world. For Fanny, the walks she took with Grandma over the hills and through the fields were walks with God, as Eunice pointed out that every tree, every flower, every bird was put there by God and served His plan and purpose.

Eunice taught Fanny and Polly that whatever happens, good or bad, is a manifestation of God's delight or wrath. She taught them that not a sparrow falls to the ground without God seeing it, that every hair on the head is numbered. She instilled in them the conviction that God is an ever-present help in trouble.

Eunice was a tower of strength to her daughter Mercy in the first years of her widowhood. Often, Mercy would become distraught by her difficulties. She had to work all day to support her child, whom she could see only at night. And she fretted about Fanny Jane, wondering what would become of this little girl who seemed so hopelessly handicapped. When Mercy collapsed upon her rough cot, weeping, Eunice would go in to her, place her hard, worn hand upon her thin shoulder and recite from a favorite hymn or quote the old Puritan adage that had been a favorite of the Puritan leader, Cotton Mather: "What can't be cured can be endured." In her nineties, Fanny Crosby still would be repeating that saying to all who came to her with their troubles.

From as early as Fanny could remember, Eunice would assemble her children and read the Bible to them. "The stories of the Holy Book came from her lips and entered my heart, and took deep root there." Eunice did not simply read from the Bible without comment but took time to explain everything in terms children could understand. Sitting in her rocking chair, she would tell them of "a kind heavenly Father Who sent His only Son, Jesus Christ, down into this world to be a Saviour and a Friend to all mankind."

Not only was Grandma a woman of the Bible, she also was "a firm believer in prayer." Prayer was essential to the Christian life, not merely as a form of mental exercise or simply in meditating on God, but as a direct communication with her loving Saviour. She taught Fanny that they should call upon God in every need and give thanks to Him for everything good that happened. She taught that there was nothing too difficult for God to do and that, whatever their need might be, He could meet it. No matter how extravagant or unlikely their request, He would grant it—*if it were good for them*. If God did not grant the request, then they should not be downcast, for He had something in store for them better than their wildest hopes and expectations. They should rejoice, therefore. The sufferings and frustrations of life could be borne patiently and cheerfully, because they were being led to something better.

> NOT ONLY WAS GRANDMA A WOMAN OF THE BIBLE, SHE ALSO WAS "A FIRM BELIEVER IN PRAYER."

Every Sunday, the Crosbys walked, like the other villagers, barefoot—shoes in hand—to the church. They went into the outlying horse sheds, tidied up, put on their shoes, and went into the meeting. In winter, the wooden structure was heated by a potbellied stove set in the center of the sanctuary. It often grew very hot inside, with two hundred persons crowding into the room, and the tobacco smoke issuing from the lips of most of the men made for an insufferable atmosphere. The sermons seemed to last forever and often were so full of tedious vagaries of Calvinist theology that people dozed throughout. At noon, the congregation went home to dinner, then promptly returned to hear more preaching. "As long as they got home in time to milk the cows, they didn't mind," recalled a resident.

There were no organ and no hymns, as such, in the "Southeast Church." Like the early Puritans, the theologians of the era did not believe in hymns of human composition; they would use only the Psalms, which were "dictated" to David directly from God. Most of the music consisted of psalms chanted in plainsong with, now and then, their metrical paraphrase by Isaac Watts, who lived and wrote a century earlier.

A deacon at "the desk" would be the only person in the room with a text. "Lining out" the psalm, he would recite one line, and the congregation would repeat it; they proceeded in this fashion until the entire psalm was chanted. This rather awkward brand of church music did not impress the child Fanny.

As a little girl, Fanny Jane was quiet and pensive but cheerful. She became staunch friends with the postman, and one of the grand events of the week was to get the mail from him each Thursday. From the age of three, on pleasant days, she would make her way with the ease of a sighted person to a large rock. There, under the watchful gaze of Grandma, she sat listening to the "voices of nature," all of which, she said, spoke a language familiar

> FANNY WAS SATISFIED WITH HER LOT, NOT REALIZING THERE WAS ANYTHING LIMITING ABOUT IT.

to her soul. Were it not for the persistent though well-meaning commiserations and "I wish you could see this or that," Fanny would not have known she was different from other children. She was quite satisfied with her lot, not realizing there was anything limiting about it.

She loved to sing. By the age of five, she knew such songs as the stately "Hail Columbia, Happy Land" and rather crude ballads like "Fourscore and Ten Old Bachelors."

Eunice and Mercy let Fanny and Polly have quite a bit of freedom. Far from keeping the little girls constantly at her side, Grandma let them roam in the vicinity of the cottage. She and Mercy even permitted them to play outside at night with the other children of Gayville. Fanny could play in the night just as well as she could in the daytime.

*Samuel Trevena Jackson, *Fanny Crosby's Story of Ninety-Four Years* (New York: Revell, 1915), p. 119.

3
WRITING VERSE

From the time it was apparent Fanny was blind, Mercy did not give up hope for a cure. After five years, aided by generous contributions from neighbors for miles around, she felt she had scraped up enough money to go to New York City to procure an appointment for Fanny to be examined by Dr. Valentine Mott—one of America's finest surgeons—of Columbia University School of Medicine.

For Fanny, the rather tedious trip by market wagon to Sing Sing and by sloop to New York was a wonderful, exciting adventure. She delighted in the sea yarns the captain told her, and she, in turn, regaled the crew and passengers with little songs she had learned. The skipper enjoyed them immensely and would send for her, tell her he was "blue," and ask her to sing for him.

But in New York, the cheerfulness waned. Mercy and Fanny were taken to Mott's offices, where an eye specialist had been called in. They confirmed the suspicion of Mercy and her parents that the "doctor" who had treated Fanny

THE CHILD COULD EXPERIENCE SOME LIGHT AND COLOR BUT LITTLE ELSE.

Jane's eyes had utterly ruined them. The poultice had burned her corneas, causing scar tissue to form. This made for a kind of vision, or lack of vision, which might be compared to looking through a glazed or iced window. The child could experience some light and color but little else. There was absolutely nothing they could do; the damage was irreversible.

The words sank into Mercy's heart like daggers. Normally stern and staid, she burst into tears. Five years of saving and scraping, five years of hope and anticipation, had come to naught.

Fanny was not totally blind. Even in her eighties, she could distinguish day from night. At that point in life, a friend remarked that she wished Fanny could see the sunlight on a particularly beautiful day. Fanny responded, "I know it. I feel it. And I see it, too!"

Little Fanny Jane had what amounted almost to a religious experience aboard the sloop returning from New York that spring afternoon in 1825.

> As I sat there on the deck, amid the glories of the departing day, the low murmur of the waves soothed my soul into a delightful peace. Their music was translated into tones that were like a human voice, and for many years their melody suggested to my imagination the call of Genius as she was struggling to be heard from her prison house in some tiny shell lying perchance on the bottom of the river.*

Back home, Grandma Crosby was there to comfort them and tell Mercy, as she was wont to do, that if the Lord did not grant a request, then it was best not to have it. She assured her distraught daughter that God would provide for little Fanny Jane and that He had a useful future for her.

About this time, Mercy was forced to move to North Salem,

six miles south of Gayville, where she was employed as a house-keeper. There was room in her employer's house for Fanny, so she decided to take her daughter with her.

North Salem was inhabited largely by Quakers, and Fanny Jane quickly learned what was called the "plain language."

Unlike gentle Grandma, Mercy was very strict. Whenever Fanny Jane was mischievous, Grandma talked to her very gently until she convinced the child of her fault and brought her to tears of peni-tence. Mercy was much freer with the rod than her mother, and this took some adjustment on the part of the child. Of her mother, she later said, "She was of the generation you *had* to mind!"

From her pictures, Mercy seems to have been the stern-visaged pioneer woman: spare and erect, with a long, bony face and hawk-like nose, hard, intense eyes, and pursed lips. She was not all disci-pline, however; she was a witty woman who liked a good time. She was frantically devoted to her handicapped daughter's welfare. To the extent her meager means would permit, Mercy would buy toys for the little girl's amusement.

Fanny played "early and late" with the other village children. The peasants of North Salem soon learned, to their amazement, that the little blind girl was certain to be a party to any childish mischief. Something of a tom-boy, Fanny learned to climb a tree "with the agility of a squirrel" and ride a horse bareback, clinging to the mane for dear life as the steed

> FANNY LEARNED TO CLIMB A TREE "WITH THE AGILITY OF A SQUIRREL."

galloped. She could climb stone walls and, when she tore her dress, she "managed to keep [the torn section] out of Mother's sight until I fancied she would not notice it, which was a rare occurrence indeed."

Grandma made it a point to visit Fanny several times a week

in North Salem. While Mercy was busy with the domestic chores of the household where she lived and worked, Eunice continued to educate her grandchild, giving her portions of the Bible to memorize when she was about eight.

Gradually, Fanny came to realize she was unlike other children. The strange, unknown phenomenon of eyesight seemed necessary for her to obtain most, if not all, of her ambitions. To be a sailor, preacher, or musician, she had to go to school. Yet the path of knowledge appeared hopelessly barred to her. It irked her to hear people say, "Oh, you cannot do this because you are blind, you know," and "You can never go there, because it would not be worthwhile; you could not see anything if you did."

Fanny in later years always insisted blind people can accomplish almost everything sighted persons can. But for the little blind girl in the Puritan hinterlands of New York State, there seemed little hope of ever realizing her ambitions. She became pensive and at times grew "very blue and depressed." It was then she would creep off alone, kneel as Grandma had taught her, and ask God whether her blindness was to exclude her from being one of His children. She would ask Him "whether, in all His great world, He had not some little place for me." Always of a mystical inclination, she felt she heard His voice saying, "Do not be discouraged, little girl. You shall some day be happy and useful, even in your blindness."

As a result of these prayers, her period of despondency passed for a season, and at age eight, she was able to compose her first attempt at verse:

Oh, what a happy child I am,
Although I cannot see!
I am resolved that in this world

Contented I will be!
How many blessings I enjoy
That other people don't!
So weep or sigh because I'm blind,
I cannot—nor I won't.

Although she had not had the "conversion experience" so essential in the Calvinism of her mother and grandmother, God was from the first a part of Fanny's life, and church in North Salem came to mean much to her. The only church was the Society of Friends. But the Quaker meeting, in which the speaker delivered his sermons in a singsong manner, gasping for breath between phrases, was quite different from the deadly Puritan services at Southeast, so they struck her fancy. The singing, especially, caught her imagination. Throughout her life she would remember the "doleful" hymns. These grave, somber hymns were common in New England at that time. They frequently were macabre poems set to eerie, fuguing tunes.

> **THE QUAKER MEETING SINGING, ESPECIALLY, CAUGHT HER IMAGINATION.**

In North Salem, as in Southeast, a great emphasis was placed on an emotional conversion experience, without which one should dread to die. There was a great emphasis on mortality and the certainty of hell for the unrepentant. Numerous hymns told of careless sinners, who were overtaken by sudden death and were lost. Even as a little girl, Fanny was revolted by scare tactics, which often hardened sinners in their unbelief rather than accomplishing the intended effect. This would impact her lifelong attitude toward religious work.

When Fanny was eight or nine, Mercy moved again, this time over the state line to nearby Ridgefield, Connecticut, where she found domestic work. She was unable to live in the same house where she worked, and Fanny was left during the day in the care of the landlady, a Mrs. Hawley. Fanny Jane carried permanent memories with her of the Quakers in North Salem. Although she soon lost the habit of calling people "thee" and "thou," at times throughout her life she loved to don Quaker dress.

Mercy and Fanny lived on the village green. Here they were once more in Presbyterian country. Mrs. Hawley was an arch Calvinist, "an old Puritan Presbyterian who took everything in the Sacred Writ as literally as the most orthodox Scotchman could do." She was not gloomy or severe, as many Puritans were,

MRS. HAWLEY SET FANNY TO THE TASK OF MEMORIZING THE ENTIRE BIBLE.

but "kind." She "loved beautiful things." Fanny was too far away from Southeast for Grandma to come regularly, but Mrs. Hawley resolved to take up Eunice's work. She set Fanny to the task of memorizing the entire Bible, giving the child a number of chapters to learn each week—often as many as five. These were repeated line by line, drilled into the little girl's head "precept upon precept."

Being young and gifted with a phenomenal memory, Fanny had no trouble mastering Genesis, Exodus, Leviticus, and Numbers, as well as the four Gospels, by the end of the year. At the end of two years, Fanny could repeat by rote not only the entire Pentateuch and all four Gospels but also many Psalms, all of Proverbs, all of Ruth, and "that greatest of all prose poems, the Song of Solomon."

This training sufficed Fanny for a lifetime. From then on she needed no one to read the Bible to her. Whenever she wanted to "read" a portion of scripture, she turned a little button in her mind, and the appropriate passage would flow through her brain like a tape recording.

When she visited Grandma in Southeast, which was fairly frequently, Eunice noted with great pleasure her progress in learning the Holy Writ. Fanny was always a champion in Bible recitation contests between the children and teenagers of Ridgefield. Whoever could repeat the most verses would win a Bible, and the Bible came to be a part of her.

Mrs. Hawley was not so strict a Calvinist as to believe there was nothing worth reading outside of Holy Writ. She had Fanny memorize portions of edifying secular works, as well as popular poems, and she taught her many "practical lessons." When she had the time, Mercy also read to Fanny, and Fanny had vivid memories of her mother reciting "with great feeling" Milton's famous sonnet "On His Blindness."

The "singing school" was very popular in New England in those days. In winter, the young people of the village were visited by a singing teacher who taught Fanny and her companions at Ridgefield from the famous *Handel and Haydn Collection* of Lowell Mason (1792–1872). This consisted mostly of songs and anthems in the style of classical European music. The *Handel and Haydn Collection* was used by the church choir, of which Fanny Jane was a member. Years later she wrote, "I can still hear some of the sweet voices of my friends reverberating through the old Presbyterian meetinghouse; the tuning-fork of the choirmaster as he 'set' the pitch; and the deep, mellow tenor of the minister as he answered the choir from the pulpit."

The Ridgefield Presbyterian Church was too poor to afford hymnals, and the deacons often lined out selections from Mason's collection in the same way those at Southeast lined out psalms. But often they invented hymns of their own, to be sung to the tunes in the *Handel and Haydn Collection*. This usually turned out horrendously, and sometimes two or three deacons were required to finish a hymn of a few stanzas.

Fanny at this time became acquainted with a tailor who was a Methodist and occasionally went to his church with him. She came to love the stately and beautiful hymns of Charles Wesley and Isaac Watts that were sung there.

> FANNY CAME TO LOVE THE STATELY HYMNS OF CHARLES WESLEY AND ISAAC WATTS.

Although Fanny was happy at times, she had recurring spells of moodiness and depression as she approached adolescence. She spent many evenings thinking and "reading" the Scriptures. Her handicap came to depress her more than it had when she was younger. She put herself more and more in competition with her comrades, just "to show the world what a little blind girl can do."

She was never to entirely outgrow this. Even as an old woman, she was always terribly anxious to demonstrate to everyone that she could do anything a sighted person could. In her nineties, she insisted that the niece with whom she stayed allow her to do the dishes.

In her eleventh and twelfth years, Fanny felt increasingly shut out of the world. She was beginning to realize a great store of knowledge lay waiting out there, but since she was blind and had no chance for an education, there seemed no way for her to tap it.

She attended the district schools occasionally, but the local school-master did not know how to instruct the blind, and she would quit in complete frustration after a few days.

In the depth of her depression, she made one of her frequent trips to Gayville to visit Grandma and Grandpa, who still lived in the house where she had been born. Eunice realized the child was deeply troubled, and toward twilight one day they had a long talk together. Grandma sat in her rocking chair and Fanny poured out her heart. Then the two of them knelt down by the side of the doughty old chair and "repeated a petition to the Kind Father." After that, Eunice went quietly downstairs, leaving Fanny alone with her thoughts.

> *The night was beautiful. I crept towards the window, and through the branches of a giant oak, that stood just outside, the soft moonlight fell upon my head like the benediction of an angel, while I knelt there and repeated over and over these simple words: "Dear Lord, please show me how I can learn like other children."*

At once, she felt "the weight of anxiety" that had burdened her heart in recent months "changed to the sweet consciousness that my prayer would be answered in due time." From then on, although Fanny often fell into depression because of the limited opportunities available to her, she treasured in her heart the confidence that ultimately the barrier that stood between her and "knowledge" would be demolished.

This was perhaps Eunice Crosby's last great gift to her grand-daughter—this prayer for knowledge that moonlit night. Soon thereafter, she fell ill.

Fanny always remembered their last meeting. On that "rosy summer evening" in 1831, Grandma sat in her favorite rocking chair, her voice a painful whisper. "Grandma's going home," she said and told the frightened child she

> "TELL ME, MY DARLING, WILL YOU MEET GRANDMA IN OUR FATHER'S HOUSE ON HIGH?"

soon would be in heaven. Fanny sobbed disconsolately before the dark silence once more was broken by the dying woman's faltering voice. She had one question to ask her beloved grandchild—her only grandchild. "Tell me, my darling, will you meet Grandma in our Father's house on high?"

Fanny could feel Eunice "looking down upon me." There was another moment of silence. Then the child overcame the lump in her throat and answered, "By the grace of God, I will." Eunice, joyful, clasped Fanny to her bosom. They bowed their heads for one last prayer. Not long afterward, Eunice Crosby—only fifty-three—died.

This last meeting was to haunt Fanny for many years. Eunice was a devout Calvinist who believed one could have assurance of salvation only through a definite, dated, emotional "conversion." She hoped Fanny would have this experience, and her deathbed words ultimately were to induce it. In truth, however, Fanny did not feel any different about salvation after leaving Grandma that last time. The fact that she had not had a datable conversion experience was to weigh upon her mind at times.

As Fanny entered her teens, she began to show obvious musical talent. With a high, sweet soprano voice, she acquired a reputation locally as a singer. She mastered the guitar to the extent that she was constantly in demand at gatherings. She became an excellent horsewoman. She also attained fame as a storyteller. She liked to invent stories of charitable bandits—the type of robbers, she commented in later years, "I have not been fortunate enough to meet. . .in real life."

It was as a poet that Fanny attained her greatest fame in Ridgefield. She wrote lyrics about events in the community. For example, a miller nearby apparently had the habit of dishonestly mixing corn meal with his flour. Fanny wrote a poem beginning:

> *There is a miller in our town,*
> *How dreadful is his case;*
> *I fear unless he does repent*
> *He'll meet with sad disgrace.*

Neighbors thought the poem so good—or the situation in need of immediate attention—that it was submitted to the editor of the nearest newspaper, the weekly *Herald of Freedom* at Danbury, whose editor was Phineas Taylor Barnum, then in his early twenties and on the threshold of his lucrative career as a showman. Barnum liked the poem and wanted to print it in full. He took an interest in Fanny and probably would have blown her up in his paper as a "blind prodigy" had not Mercy intervened. She astutely recognized the youthful Barnum's inclination for exhibiting things and people. Fanny, who did not like Barnum, wrote years later that had Barnum had his way, she might "have held an uncomfortable position in his hall of fame."

Following the practice of the day, in which the chief theme of literary endeavors was death, Fanny tried her hand at writing obituary verse. For a while, whenever anybody in the neighborhood died, Fanny would "cause my muse to shed a few sympathetic tears."

Later, she felt ashamed of these youthful elegies. "How glad I am that none of these is preserved!"

When Fanny wrote a poem called "The Moaning of the Wind for the Flowers," Mrs. Hawley liked it so well she sent a copy to Sylvanus in Gayville. Grandpa Crosby was enthusiastic about the poem and wrote Mrs. Hawley for copies of more of his granddaughter's works. He praised her work and hailed her to his friends and neighbors as a "comer." But he did not want to "spoil her and make her proud," so he instructed Mercy to communicate to Fanny none of his enthusiasm. It was not until years later that Fanny learned how proud her grandfather had been.

In 1834, Mercy decided to move back to North Salem. In Ridgefield, Fanny had come to know the Bible by heart, received her first rudimentary musical training, and met someone who would be most influential to her future. One of the children with whom she played on the green was Sylvester Main, three years her senior. "Vet" Main and his son Hugh's publishing house would publish nearly six thousand of Fanny's hymns and be one of the principal means by which her works would gain access to America's hearts and homes.

*Frances J. Crosby, *Memories of Eighty Years* (Boston: James H. Earle, 1906), p. 9.

4
NEW YORK INSTITUTION FOR THE BLIND

At fourteen, Fanny, small in stature, was a lively little girl with jet black curls. Although not especially attractive, she had a personality of rare intensity and vitality that tended to express itself in passionate emotions—violent sorrow as well as violent joy. Whatever she did—horseback riding, playing the guitar, singing, telling stories, writing poetry—she did with a fierce passion that was almost more than her meager frame could bear. It was to be so throughout her life.

She still attended the district school in spurts, but the harried schoolmaster, with more students than he could handle, had no time for the special attention and training she needed. After attending classes a few days, Fanny, in despair, would drop out.

But in November 1834, Mercy read to her a circular about the newly founded New York Institution for the Blind. Fanny clapped her hands and cried, "O, thank God! He has answered my prayer, just as I knew He could!" Seventy years of joy and sorrow later, she still could describe that day as the happiest of her life.

She left by stagecoach the morning of March 3, 1835. Fanny was "thoroughly unnerved" and trembled so badly she could scarcely dress. The lump in her throat allowed her to swallow only a few morsels of the breakfast Mercy had prepared. Forcing back sobs, she hurried from the house. The stage lurched forward on its route to Norwalk, Connecticut, where Fanny and her traveling companion—a woman whose name we do not know—would take a steamer to Manhattan.

The woman tried to get Fanny to talk, but she languished in silence. At length, the woman said severely, "Fanny, if you don't want to go to New York, we will get out at the next station and take the returning stage home. Your mother will be lonesome without you, anyway."

Fanny realized a return to the frustrating, unrewarding life as the village bard in a rustic Yankee community was not a viable option. She decided to "cross the Rubicon" by staying aboard at the next station. "Had I returned to my mother that morning," she wrote, "I would have cast away my pearl of great price, for it is not probable that I should ever have been brave enough to start again for the Institution."

Funded by the state and by public contributions, the Institution had been established four years earlier with three students. It was only the second such establishment in the United States, coming two years after the Institution for the Blind in Boston. The instructors sought to draw support by staging at schools and churches exhibitions of the pupils' work. In those days, not many people believed the blind could be successfully educated.

> **IN THOSE DAYS, NOT MANY PEOPLE BELIEVED THE BLIND COULD BE SUCCESSFULLY EDUCATED.**

The authorities also sent flyers to all parts of the state. The number of pupils increased so rapidly—thirty, by the year 1835—that the instructors were able to lease a private mansion on a pleasant country estate shaded by old willow trees. John Denison Russ, a physician and Yale graduate, was then the superintendent of the estate on Manhattan's West Side—at that time situated in the country.

Dr. Russ (1801–1881) was much loved by his students. He invented a phonetic alphabet and worked diligently to perfect the system of raised characters and maps that Louis Braille had developed several years earlier in France. Russ came to the Institution when it was founded and served without pay for the first two years. Despite a busy schedule and heavy responsibilities, he was never too busy to take a personal interest in the pupils. He taught Bible classes and read to them from his favorite poet, Lord Byron.

Fanny arrived March 7. During her first days, she was simply homesick. The first night, she was led to the little room that was to be hers. "Everything was strange" and nothing was in the place where she was accustomed to find it at home. Thoroughly disconcerted, she was sitting on her trunk, trying to be brave and forcing back the tears, when the matron of the institution entered.

"Fanny," said the motherly Quakeress, throwing herself about the girl's thin body, "I guess thee has never been away from home before."

"No, ma'am," said Fanny weakly. "Please excuse me. I must cry."

And she did, loud and long, until another pupil succeeded in comforting her.

Soon, the once-forbidding Institution became "my happy home" where, in the next two decades, she experienced "the brightest joys I e'er have known." Outgoing, she rapidly made friends. With her keen mind, she quickly mastered her lessons in English, grammar, science, music, history, philosophy, astronomy, and political economy. The lessons were given in the form of lectures and readings, after which the pupils were expected to answer detailed questions on the text they had heard. The next day they were to paraphrase the entire lesson. Fanny learned unusually well; to the day of her death, she was able to recite the entire text of *Brown's Grammar*.

She was "in love with" grammar, philosophy, astronomy, and political science, but she had trouble with Braille and math. She was taught to read the Bible, *The Pilgrim's Progress,* and Coleridge's "Rime of the Ancient Mariner" in Braille, but apparently did so very slowly and laboriously. This woman who could recognize a person instantaneously by the touch of the hand claimed she could never master the raised alphabet; this she blamed on her guitar playing, which callused her fingertips. After she left the Institution, she rarely used Braille. She relied more on her memory and training. Whenever she wanted to read a book, she would have someone read it to her; after one reading, the contents were stamped on her remarkable memory.

Mathematics was a "great monster." It was taught on metal slates with holes; the students could count and realize the numbers as they worked. She managed to learn addition and subtraction. Multiplication was harder, and when it came to division, Fanny balked entirely. "I have never been a very good hater," she said later, "even when the best material was provided for the purpose; but I found myself an adept at the art of loathing, when it came to the Science of Numbers."

Advanced students sometimes were assigned to teach newer ones. Anna Smith, who later became one of Fanny's most intimate friends, was trying to teach her arithmetic. She soon realized Fanny had no aptitude for figures and told Russ so. The superintendent wisely decided Fanny could better spend her time in other studies, so he excused her from taking more arithmetic.

"From that hour I was a new creature," Fanny recalled. "What a nightmare I was escaping!"

Fanny's favorite avocation continued to be writing poetry. She tried to imitate the leading poets of the day. Her schoolmates, in turn, tried to imitate Fanny's poetry. She was considered adept enough to compose the words to a march by Anthony Reiff, a sighted music teacher. The march was sung by the Institution choir at the laying of the cornerstone for the new school building in 1837.

FANNY'S FAVORITE AVOCATION CONTINUED TO BE WRITING POETRY.

But Fanny's instructors noticed she was developing a "swelled head." This was brought to the attention of Dr. Silas Jones, who had replaced Russ as superintendent in 1836. He called Fanny into his office one morning. She expected to be asked to write another poem "to the honor of some distinguished person or event." She was flabbergasted when Jones instead delivered a grave lecture. "Do not think too much about rhymes and the praises that come from them," he said. "Store your mind with useful knowledge and think more of what you can *be* than of how you can *appear.*"

His words, Fanny recalled, "were bombshells in the camp of my self-congratulatory thoughts." Hot tears came to her eyes. But she recovered, threw her arms around his neck, and kissed him on the forehead. "You talked to me as my father would have talked if he were living, and I thank you for it."

In the coming weeks and months, the quality of her poetry rapidly improved. Before she was twenty, she was the Institution's most promising pupil. She had become proficient at the piano and organ and was reputed to be one of the finest harpists in America.

These years at the Institution were filled with hard work and pleasant diversion. Though respected for her progress and abilities, she was a high-spirited girl, sure to be part of any mischief.

To help support her mother, she decided to become a teacher. Although not one of the regular instructors, she was assigned to teach some of the subjects and skills to newcomers, just as Anna Smith had tried to teach arithmetic to her.

Dr. Jones was concerned that Fanny was devoting too much of her time to poetry, to the exclusion of her other studies. He wanted to determine if she had real talent or if she were one of those people who write rhymes because they are poetry lovers. He forbade her to write any poetry for three months. He reasoned that if she were a real poet, she would not be able to withstand this "trial by fire," but if she were merely a dilettante, the enforced layoff would not faze her.

She became so despondent she could do nothing. After six weeks of failure in her lessons, Jones called her to his office and demanded the reason for the poor work. Fanny's only excuse was that poetry occupied her thoughts so much it was impossible to keep her mind on other things when she was forbidden to write it. Convinced she was a real poet, Jones agreed to let her write poetry if she would pay more attention to the lectures.

Soon afterward, the Institution was visited by George Combe (1778–1858), a Scottish phrenologist. A believer in character determination based on the shape and texture of the skull, Combe studied Fanny's head and remarked, "Why, here is a poetess! Give her every advantage. Read the best books to her, and teach her to appreciate the best poetry."

So Jones found Fanny a teacher in poetic composition: Hamilton Murray, who claimed that while he could not write poetry, he could teach others to do so. Murray read long passages of poetry to Fanny and required her to memorize them. He taught the proper use of rhyme, rhythm, and meter, pointed out the defects of her poetry, and had her imitate the works of well-known poets.

He was very strict. From him, she learned not only poetic technique but rapidity of composition. It was owing to his discipline that in later years she was able to whip up as many as a dozen hymns a day. For all Murray did, she was eternally grateful.

> **SHE WAS ABLE TO WHIP UP AS MANY AS A DOZEN HYMNS A DAY.**

5
EXHIBIT NUMBER ONE

While Fanny was becoming the Institution's most promising student, her mother was beginning a new life. In 1836, Mercy left North Salem to live with her brother Joseph and his family on the outskirts of Bridgeport. There she met and married Thomas Morris, a widower with three children, in February 1838. The next year, at age forty, she bore him a daughter they named Wilhelmina. The child died in infancy, to the terrible grief of all, including Fanny. The following year, Mercy bore Thomas another daughter. They named her Julia and called her Jule.

An ardent Democrat, Fanny spent much of her time in the autumn of 1840 writing verse directed against the Whig rival, the much-beloved General William Henry Harrison. Despite her efforts, Harrison was elected, and when he died after only a month in office, Fanny was content to bury the hatchet with verse. Her conventional Early American romantic elegy—perhaps because it was composed by a blind woman—received considerable attention through its publication in the *New York Herald*. A proud Grandfather Sylvanus, still living in Gayville, walked four miles each way to a town to buy a newspaper.

After this, Fanny's reputation as "the Blind Poetess" grew. Students at the Institution frequently were invited to give demonstrations at schools, churches, and elsewhere to show what the blind were capable of accomplishing. They gave exhibitions of Braille readings in geography, history, arithmetic, and other subjects, as well as songs and recitations. Fanny sang and played the piano, organ, and harp. The exhibition always was closed by one of her "original poetical addresses." These pieces, filled with stock poetic diction, were written not at some unbidden impulse to reflect the outpouring of her soul, but at the request of the Institution managers to obtain monetary support. There was no extraordinary merit in most of these poems, although the form and style were impeccable.

Her listeners were interested not so much in her poetic gifts but in her educability. She was the poet-in-residence, so to speak, of the Institution, and as she gradually attained a reputation, it was as much for what she symbolized as for what she wrote.

SHE WAS THE POET-IN-RESIDENCE OF THE INSTITUTION.

Nevertheless, listeners were moved by certain attributes of her poetry, notably her descriptive powers. Fanny was much more impressive when she recited at soirées than on more official occasions; for in the less formal atmosphere, she could recite poems she actually had been inspired to write. In some of her blank verse, her fantastic descriptive powers were evident.

Fanny was called to recite before many of the distinguished visitors who came to the Institution in the early days, curious about this new phenomenon of educating the blind. President John Tyler, along with the mayor of New York City and the entire city council, suddenly appeared one June day. The new superintendent, Peter Vroom, rushed into Fanny's room and told her about the visitors waiting in the reception room. With fifteen minutes' notice, Fanny prepared a poetic greeting for the president of the United States. At the appointed time, the poem was ready. Fanny recited it before the eminent visitors and then sang a song.

New York governor William Henry Seward, later Lincoln's secretary of state, also visited the Institution, as did prominent visitors from overseas. From France in 1843 came Henri Gratien, Count Bertrand (1773–1844), Napoleon's old field marshal who had shared his master's exile on St. Helena before being pardoned. Fanny recited a poem written in honor of the elderly soldier. Bertrand was deeply moved.

The Institution was graced by a visit from William Cullen Bryant, then forty-nine years old and America's leading poet. The author of "Thanatopsis" and "To a Waterfowl" appeared at a soirée. Fanny had no idea Bryant was acquainted with her poetry, but to her astonishment, he recognized her as "the Blind Poetess" and commended her efforts. He said she had real talent and potential and encouraged her to continue writing. "He never knew," Fanny wrote later, "how much good he did by those few words."

Fanny became acquainted with many public people, and she formed several warm friendships with her colleagues. Among these was Imogene Hart, who became a musician. There was also her roommate, Alice Holmes, a year younger than Fanny, who had contracted smallpox, which left her blind at age nine; Miss Holmes, as "the Blind Poet of Jersey City," published several volumes of verse. Perhaps Fanny's fondest attachment during her Institution years was to Anna Smith, who had tried to teach her mathematics.

In the summer of 1842, the board of managers decided that twenty of the Institution's best students should tour central New York State to demonstrate the educability of the blind and induce parents of blind children to send them to the New York school. Of course, "the Blind Poetess" was a member of the company. They traveled west by what Fanny called "the highway of waves," the Erie Canal. Mule-drawn packet boats plied their way, laden with freight and passengers. In one of these, Fanny and her colleagues traveled to Schenectady, Rome, Utica, Syracuse, Rochester, and Buffalo. At each city and in some of the towns along the way, a reception was held. The mayor and prominent citizens would speak, and hundreds of townsfolk would gather, attracted by the strange tales of blind people being taught useful trades. The pupils sang, danced, gave speeches, and described their school. Fanny played the piano and harp, sang, and recited poems.

> **FANNY PLAYED THE PIANO AND HARP, SANG, AND RECITED POEMS.**

The following summer, Fanny was chosen for another group tour of New York State. She found it tedious being "exhibit number one," traveling from town to town, hearing pompous mayors give speeches and condescending officials make flowery pledges of support that were never meant to be. People would ask that infuriating question: "How long have you been—er, ah—that way?" Frequently, they would ask how blind people managed to get food to their mouths when they ate; Fanny liked to respond that they would take a string and tie one end to the table leg and the other to their tongues and work the food up to their mouths along the string.

Several weeks of answering such questions and composing "original poetical addresses" to be read at each stop left her completely exhausted.

The tour brought Fanny one benefit that would not be fulfilled for fifteen years. At Oswego, a woman was so impressed, she decided the Institution was the place to send her blind son.

She introduced the boy to Fanny and asked her to take him under her personal charge when he arrived. "Take good care of my boy," Mary Van Alstine said—not realizing that Fanny would take such good care of little Alexander that he would marry her!

That fall, Fanny was a regular instructor at the Institution. She taught rhetoric, grammar, and Roman and American history. It took much work to prepare for her courses. Although exhausted at the end of the day, she frequently stayed up until 2 a.m. composing poetry.

The strain of her course work, coming at the end of the summer tour, was devastating. The Institution doctor, J. W. G. Clements, realized she needed rest and recommended she forgo meeting her classes for a while and skip an upcoming visit to Washington, D.C., during which she was to recite poetry before members of Congress. Fanny yearned to go to Washington, and Clements finally decided she would worry herself into a fever if left behind.

Her joy at being allowed to make the trip turned to apprehension when she learned the great importance being pinned on her presentation. The managers wanted Congress to pass legislation to create institutions for the blind and provide free education to blind children in every state of the Union. They hoped Fanny's poetry would pull on the congressional heartstrings.

On the evening of January 24, 1844, seventeen pupils from the Institution gave their "concert and exhibition." Climaxing a program of musical performances and grammar and math examinations, Fanny recited her thirteen-stanza poem. The congressmen burst into applause so loud it sounded like thunder to Fanny and frightened her.

They insisted she give an encore. She decided

FANNY RECITED HER THIRTEEN-STANZA POEM. THE CONGRESSMEN BURST INTO APPLAUSE.

on an elegy written the previous summer upon the sudden death of Hugh Legare, Tyler's "lamented secretary of state," who had suffered a heart attack while laying the cornerstone for the new Bunker Hill monument. By the time she finished, the congressmen were weeping audibly. Legare's sister met Fanny at the chamber door and gave her a beautiful ring. John Quincy Adams, the crusty ex-president, wrung her hand.

But for all its weeping, Congress did not pass the Institution's proposal.

Almost in a state of collapse on their return to New York, Fanny did not meet any of her classes that spring but spent the time working on the first volume of poetry she would publish. By April, *The Blind Girl and Other Poems* was ready. The 160-page book contained a preface written by her friend and mentor, Hamilton Murray. Since the book was being published in part to raise money for the Institution, Murray used the preface to make a pitch for the reader's purse. He exaggerated ominously of the poet's "declining health."

The publishers wanted a daguerreotype of the author for the frontispiece. Sitting for a picture was something of an ordeal for Fanny. The exposure required several minutes, during which she was required to sit stock-still.

Interestingly, this first photograph is the only known picture that shows Fanny smiling! She does not appear to be in ill health. She stood only four feet nine inches tall and claimed never to have weighed as much as a hundred pounds, but of all the photos taken during her life, this one shows her at her heaviest.

A beauty she was not. The photo indicates a rather long horse face and a small, blunt nose. The lips, parted in the smile, reveal somewhat prominent front teeth with a gap between them. Dark, rectangular spectacles entirely obscure the sightless eyes. The ears are "jug-handled." The hair is thick, dark, and wavy, parted in the middle, and pulled backward in curls that hang to the shoulders.

The book enjoyed moderately good sales, and the name of Fanny Crosby grew in familiarity. But was she a hack writer, or did she have true genius?

"The Blind Poetess" may have been noted more for being blind than for being a poet. She was seen by most people as a symbol of what the blind could do, and her poetry was viewed simply as a manifestation of that larger accomplishment. However, even had her poems been written by a sighted person, they would have claimed attention.

"THE BLIND POETESS" MAY HAVE BEEN NOTED MORE FOR BEING BLIND THAN FOR BEING A POET.

It is not known how many secular poems she wrote, but they probably number in the thousands. She wrote verse for every occasion in her life and that of her friends: weddings, anniversaries, birthdays, funerals, church events, national events, tea parties. Whenever she left the house of a friend after a visit, she bestowed upon her host a few lines of verse. In normal daily conversation, she was likely to use poetic or quasipoetic expressions, like: "In the Institution I touched the poetic garment of Mrs. Sigourney, sat long at the feet of Bayard Taylor, slaked my thirsty soul at the living streams of Frances Ridley Havergal, and drank deeply from the chalices of Longfellow, Whittier, Holmes, and Lowell." She also was likely to burst into outright verse, such as her after-dinner remark: "Now just as sure as I'm a sinner, I know I've had a very good dinner."

She was a regular contributor to the poetry columns of various

New York newspapers. Ultimately, she would publish four books of poetry: *The Blind Girl* (1844), *Monterey and Other Poems* (1851), *A Wreath of Columbia's Flowers* (1858), and *Bells at Evening* (1897).

The quality of her verse varies wildly. Many of her published poems are weak and undistinguished—even blatantly bad. Yet the same brain that produced some appallingly banal lines was also capable of writing this excerpt from "Samson with the Philistines":

> *His hair had grown. He knew it. But his eyes—*
> *Would they return? Would he again behold*
> *Or sun or moon or stars or human face?*
> *O, heaven! In all our catalogue of woes*
> *Can there be one that so afflicts the mind*
> *And rends the very fibres of the heart*
> *Like that which comes, when in our riper years,*
> *We lose, and by a single stroke of Thine,*
> *That sense, which of all others, most we prize,*
> *That glorious avenue through which we range*
> *The fields of science, poesy, and art,*
> *And trace Thee in Thy excellence divine*
> *Where Thou hast left Thy Name in living light*
> *On Truth's immortal page, Thy Holy Book?*
> *O, to be left at midday in the dark!*
> *To wander on and on in moonless night!*
> *To know the windows of the soul are closed,*
> *And closed till opened in eternity!*
> *They who have felt can tell how deep the gloom,*
> *And only they who in their souls have learned*
> *To walk by faith and lean on God for help,*
> *To such a lot can e'er be reconciled.*

Her great friend, Henry Adelbert White (1880–1951), himself a poet and for many years a university English professor, admired Fanny's poetry and considered her a first-class writer. George Henry Sandison (1850–1900), a literary critic and editor, admitted in 1897 that in many of the gospel hymns, the literary critic could not "discover at once the full-orbed genius of a poet," but he maintained Fanny was "naturally a classical poet" who wrote excellent secular verse.

> FANNY WAS "NATURALLY A CLASSICAL POET" WHO WROTE EXCELLENT SECULAR VERSE.

She wrote in the mode of the popular poets of her day. Much of their poetry seems unexceptional. But the average reader did not expect poets to say much that was profound; poets were to stimulate the emotions by treating the familiar themes of home, motherhood, unrequited love, patriotism, grief, and death. The test of a poet's success was how readily and how much the reader was made to cry.

In the nineteenth century, the Chatauqua assemblies, which in many ways filled the role of modern-day television, frequently opened and closed with poetic addresses. When a distinguished person visited a town or institution, a local poet usually was enlisted to greet them in verse. When a famous person died, numerous eulogies appeared in local papers or were read at the funeral or wake.

It was in such a literary era that Fanny Crosby wrote most of her secular poems, and like other poets of the day, she intended to put common sentimental themes to rhyme. She could arouse the emotions. She dealt in everyday actions, wringing the heartstrings not so much by high-flown language as by homey examples and allusions.

She never achieved fame as a major poet. She had precious few opportunities to compose serious verse. She was expected to be "the Blind Poetess," drawing attention to the Institution and to the plight of the blind. Her role was that of an entertainer through whom the Institution could raise money.

She was content with the role. Grateful to the Institution for providing an excellent education without cost, she was willing to do anything she could to help its cause, even if it meant sacrificing genuine poetic potential.

6
THE COMMON TOUCH

Success as "the Blind Poetess" did not go to Fanny's head. One afternoon, she was asked to show a visitor through the Institution. During the tour, the man happened to catch sight of a stack of volumes of *The Blind Girl*. "Oh, here is the Fanny Crosby book," he said enthusiastically. "You must know her, I suppose." Rather than chide him for not recognizing such an eminent person of letters on sight (after all, her picture was in the front of the book), she merely nodded.

"Is she a likable girl?"

"Oh, no!" she said, shaking her black curls gravely. "Far from it!"

Buying one of the books, he left Fanny his card. When he was gone, she learned her visitor had been none other than Johann Ludwig Tellkampf, an eminent professor at Columbia College.

Through sales of *The Blind Girl*, the name of Fanny Crosby became familiar in many households of New York and nearer New England. How proud her grandfather would have been—but alas, Sylvanus now lay buried in the little cemetery at Doanesburg.

Overworked, her constitution still suffered alarmingly. Dr. Clements, fearing a collapse, ordered Fanny to spend the summer at home, in complete rest.

Events both joyful and tragic had transpired there since her last visit two years previously. On Christmas Day 1843, Mercy had presented her husband with a living gift: their third daughter, Carolyn.

In spring, disaster struck. Thomas Morris abandoned Mercy and moved to Illinois to join Joseph Smith, the "Prophet" of the Church of Jesus Christ of Latter-Day Saints. Thomas took with him two of the children by his first wife. But fifteen-year-old William, his oldest child, wanted no part of the adventure and hid until his father had left, then remained behind with his stepmother. Thomas ended his days in Utah as a gardener for Brigham Young, Smith's successor.

It was on the heels of this tragic desertion that Fanny returned to her mother's household. The rest and change of environment was just what she needed. In September, Fanny returned to New York in perfect health, to the amazement of her colleagues.

Fanny quickly got back into her routine of teaching and reciting her poetry for the dignitaries who visited the Institution. During the summer, *The Blind Girl* had circulated farther among the literary circles of the East.

One celebrity who previously had visited the Institution and now took a new interest in Fanny was Horace Greeley (1811–1872), the famous newspaper editor. He invited her to contribute poems to his newspaper, the *New York Tribune*. It was an influential liberal paper, backing the Whig party and social reform. Although a Democrat, Fanny was progressive in her political and social outlook and admired Greeley and most of the ideas his paper supported. She accepted his offer. "I hardly knew whether I walked or flew to my room that night," she wrote. "I was so proud at having been recognized as a poet by such a great genius as Horace Greeley."

By this time, Fanny was contributing to several periodicals: James Gordon Bennett's *New York Herald,* the *Saturday Emporium,* the *Saturday Evening Post,* and the Clinton *Signal.*

That fall, former president Martin Van Buren took her out to dinner. A man of fashion and elegance, Van Buren was charmed by his young guest, and Fanny became attached to the middle-aged politician, who was in his sixties. "Down to his dying day," she later wrote, "he was one of my closest friends." What she meant by "closest friends" is questionable. Despite her piety, Fanny was something of a name dropper, even in old age, and often referred to prominent persons as "close friends" when she had met them only a few times.

> FORMER PRESIDENT MARTIN VAN BUREN TOOK HER OUT TO DINNER.

The next year, Fanny had the honor of meeting her fourth president, the newly inaugurated James K. Polk. Polk and his staff made an official visit to the Institution, and Fanny was drafted, as usual, to recite a welcoming poem.

In April 1846, Fanny was again in Washington and once more in presidential society. Delegations from the institutions for the blind in Boston, Philadelphia, and New York appeared before Congress, again on behalf of those who wanted to establish free institutions for the blind in every state. The effort was unsuccessful, but Fanny renewed her acquaintance with President Polk when, at a White House dinner for her and her colleagues, she sang a song she had dedicated to him. She also met again former president John Quincy Adams, then a respected member of Congress. And she had been introduced to many other congressmen, including two future presidents, James Buchanan and Andrew Johnson.

Back at the Institution, Fanny sometimes grew weary of her position as poet laureate. It was annoying to be "expected, whenever anything unusual happened, to embalm the event in rhyme and measure." Yet this was what her public demanded. For instance, Fanny—or "Fan," as she now was often called—was obliged to celebrate in verse the killing of a mouse by a girl at the Institution. On another occasion, she was asked to write about an incident in which a teacher at the Institution awoke to find a mouse in his long, disheveled hair. Though mildly irritated to be asked to write such nonsense, Fanny would write it, even if it meant sacrificing time she otherwise would have spent writing genuine poetry.

Whenever she heard of the death of a prominent person, she automatically sat down and compiled an elegy. In February 1848, John Quincy Adams succumbed to a brain hemorrhage. Fanny composed an elegy entitled "Weep Not for the Dead" (in which she employed the pagan device of representing the soul of the dead man in the form of a bird).

Among those who took part in his funeral two weeks later were Henry Clay, the popular senator and presidential hopeful from Kentucky. The following day, Clay paid a call at the Institution for the Blind. James Chamberlain, the current superintendent, gave him a long-winded introduction at a formal welcome. Chamberlain introduced Fanny to the senator, and as she recited a poem of greeting, a *Herald* reporter noted that Clay seemed "much affected." When she finished, Clay took her arm in his and led her to the front of the speaker's platform. He told the audience, "This is not the only poem for which I am indebted to this lady. Six months ago, she sent me some lines on the death of my dear son."

Indeed, Fanny had written "On the Death of Colonel Clay" in memory of Henry Clay Jr., a casualty in the Mexican War. Friends had persuaded her to send a copy to the senator. His voice trembled as he told the audience about the poem. Then, "he did not speak for some minutes, while both of us stood there, weeping," Fanny recalled.

Two weeks later, General Winfield Scott, the hero of the Mexican War, visited the students unexpectedly. While Chamberlain feverishly struggled to prepare a welcoming program for "Old Fuss and Feathers," Fanny was called upon to entertain him in the parlor. Fanny had a lifelong fascination with war—which seems incongruous with everything else we know of her gentleness and sensitivity. Even when she was an old woman, she remained proud of the fact she'd had relatives in every military conflict in which the United States had been involved, from the American Revolution down to the Spanish-American War and the Boxer Rebellion. She had enthusiastically supported President Polk's policies in the Mexican War and had written several poems celebrating the frightful conflict, with lines like these:

> *In the halls of Mont'zuma*
> *now revel the grave,*
> *'Tis thine arm that hath*
> *conquered the Mexican slave,*
> *Thou hast burned thy sword*
> *in the enemy's breast,*
> *They quailed at thy glance—*
> *Thou has laid them to rest.*

She recited some of these lines to Scott, and they were too much even for the military man. He was repelled.

Fanny gushed, "How did it seem when you really found yourself in the halls of Montezuma, General? Did you feel like shouting?"

The general growled, "No. I felt like falling on my knees and thanking God for the victory."

He went on to tell Fanny, "War is a terrible thing—demoralizing, degrading, cruel, devastating in all its immediate effects."

Fanny never forgot the general's comments. It puzzled her to hear so highly esteemed a military hero speak with such distaste of his livelihood.

That summer, the president himself visited the Institution unexpected and unattended. In ill health, Polk, who was not seeking reelection, told the startled administrators he did not want a reception. He happened to be in the city and had come to the campus simply for a rest. He remembered the tranquil beauty of the grounds. Since Fanny and Polk had met, Chamberlain asked her to accompany the president on a leisurely stroll.

Though she walked with presidents, Fanny never lost the common touch. Throughout these years as the premier attraction of the New York Institution for the Blind, she was loved by her pupils as a devoted teacher and an affectionate friend.

> **THOUGH SHE WALKED WITH PRESIDENTS, FANNY NEVER LOST THE COMMON TOUCH.**

7
PERSONAL REVIVAL

While 1848 had been a year for eminent visitors at the Institution, 1849 saw another visitor, a less friendly one. The guest whose visit made the greatest impact on the Institution—and on much of America—was the ghastly pestilence from the Orient.

The Pale Horse—cholera—began galloping through Russia, India, and Persia in 1846. Twenty thousand died in Persia in a few months' time. By the spring of 1849, seventy thousand were reported dead in Britain. Americans were gripped in fear, awaiting the plague's approach.

At the Institution, Fanny and others calmed the more terrified residents with assurances that the future was in God's hands. Fanny impressed upon her pupils, as it had been impressed upon her years before by her grandmother, that "the good Friend above that had been so merciful to us thus far would not desert us now; that He would do all things best for us, both in this world and in the next. . . . And so we prayed—and waited."

The epidemic was carried by passenger ship in December 1848, to New Orleans, where thirty-five hundred died. The Pale Specter invisibly permeated the sailing ships, flatboats, and steamers that left the southern port. In May, it broke out in the East.

Superintendent Chamberlain thought it best to dismiss students from the Institution for an early vacation, because the disease was much less severe in the country than in heavily populated areas. But since some pupils, for different reasons, were unable to return to their homes Fanny and certain other faculty members remained "convinced that God would take care of us and that we could be of some help."

On May 17, three people died of cholera in a lower Manhattan tenement. The disease had struck New York.

Fanny volunteered as a nurse to help the Institution's physician, Dr. Clements. Her time was occupied making "cholera pills"—two-thirds calomel and one-third opium.

By mid-July, five hundred to eight hundred a week were dying in Manhattan. Later that month, a school one block from the Institution was turned into a cholera hospital. Here, Dr. Clements and Fanny labored to relieve the stricken. Ten pupils from the Institution died.

Toiling in the hospital, Fanny became increasingly overwhelmed. "The horrors of the situation grew upon us day by day," she wrote. A half-century later, she still could hear "the harsh cry of the truckman, 'Bring out your dead!'" When her patients died, they usually were removed as quickly and quietly as possible, but "I remember my fright at sometimes stumbling over coffins in the halls, on my way from room to room."

> TOILING IN THE HOSPITAL, FANNY BECAME INCREASINGLY OVERWHELMED.

In the midst of the epidemic, Fanny was asked to welcome with a poem the white-haired Irish priest Father Theobald Mathew, who had chosen this dreadful time to observe the Institution for the Blind. Father Mathew had a tremendous reputation on both sides of the Atlantic as an evangelist. He was a great advocate of temperance; during his lifetime he had led nearly seven hundred thousand to sign pledges of total abstinence from alcohol.

He also was said to have worked many miracles of healing. His visit was "like the visit of an angel to a house of death," Fanny reported. The priest was impressed by Fanny's great piety, and when he left, he laid his hands on her head to bless her. "His touch seemed to me like that of a saint who had been permitted to leave his abode in heaven for one single moment to cheer the desolate children of earth." It was perhaps from Father Mathew that Fanny acquired her great love and respect for the Roman Catholic Church.

Fanny was unable to withstand the horrors of that summer. Already, she had been sent to Brooklyn for a three-day rest, and shortly after the visit, she felt certain she herself was coming down with cholera. She liberally dosed herself with the cholera pills she had been making and went to bed. By the next morning all her symptoms were gone, but when Chamberlain learned his most valued teacher had almost contracted the pestilence, he ordered her to take a vacation. So in early August, Fanny left for Bridgeport, to remain until fall.

Preoccupied by thoughts of death and desolation, she fell into a state of deep depression. She tried to distract herself by organizing a new collection, *Monterey and Other Poems*. Her mental state is evident in the preface, in which she spoke of "health sadly impaired" and an "inability to discharge those duties from which I have hitherto derived a maintenance."

PREOCCUPIED BY THOUGHTS OF DEATH, SHE FELL INTO A STATE OF DEEP DEPRESSION.

During the abbreviated semester of 1849–1850, she was able to meet few classes. She suffered from no specific disease, but from "sadness and depression." This was caused in part by her anxiety about her eternal destiny. Had she succumbed to the pestilence, where would she be now? Would she have been ready to meet her Maker?

The last meeting with her grandmother weighed deeply on her mind. Fanny had not experienced the distinct emotional "conversion experience" so important to her ancestor. She began to doubt her faith. She doubted her life was totally consecrated to the service of God, as she felt it should be. Although she had never lost her profound faith in God and His goodness, she grew increasingly convinced that she had not taken seriously enough the lecture Superintendent Jones had given her long before, warning her of letting success go to her head. She had enjoyed being acclaimed as "the Blind Poetess," but she came to question its worth: What did it mean in the face of death?

Fanny attended a series of revivals that fall at the Methodist Broadway Tabernacle on Thirtieth Street. Fanny, reared in a cold and colorless Calvinistic Presbyterian church, was drawn to the Methodists' warm and lively services and their fervent and comparatively cheerful hymn singing. As early as 1839, she had attended Methodist "class meetings" at the Eighteenth Street Church, where the pious gathered to sing, pray, "testify," and read scripture in free-flowing, informal meetings that appealed to many young persons. Often the leader, without warning, would call upon someone to testify, and that person would talk about all God had done for him or her.

In her teens and twenties, Fanny had attended class meetings twice a week, once at Eighteenth Street and once at the Institution, where the Methodist church sent a man every Thursday evening to lead a meeting. Nevertheless, she had "grown somewhat indifferent to the means of grace," and she attended simply to provide the worshippers with music for their meetings. She played "on the condition that they should not call on me to speak." A decade later, Fanny was still afraid to "testify" in the meetings.

Fanny had a close friend named Theodore Camp, a teacher of industrial science at the Institution, who suggested she go with him to the revivals at the Broadway Tabernacle. At first, she apparently hesitated. Then one night she had a vivid and disconcerting dream. "It seemed that the sky had been cloudy for a number of days and finally, someone came to me and said that Mr. Camp desired to see me at once. Then I thought I entered the room and found him very ill."

The "dying" Camp (who was to live for another half-century) asked if she would meet him in heaven after their deaths.

"Yes, I will," Fanny said, "God helping me." This, it will be remembered, was the response she had given her dying grandmother.

In the dream, just before he died, Camp admonished, "Remember, you promised a dying man!"

Fanny recorded:

Then the clouds seemed to roll from my spirit, and I awoke from the dream with a start. I could not forget those words, "Will you meet me in heaven?," and, although my friend was perfectly well, I began to consider whether I could really meet him, or any other acquaintance, in the Better Land, if called to do so.

Fanny was convinced that as things stood, she could not. Although from all indications she had never ceased to be a deeply religious woman, she was certain she had denied the faith in which she had been reared and had allowed it to take second place in her life to literary and social concerns. She felt there was something terribly lacking in her spiritual life.

She began to attend the revivals with Camp every evening in the autumn of 1850. In those days, the service was highlighted by a long, emotional sermon, punctuated by cries of "Amen!" and "Hallelujah!" There were inarticulate cries, convulsive sobbings, and ecstatic outbursts. It was not uncommon for the frenzied worshippers to leap from their seats and run about or fall on the floor.

When the preacher concluded the sermon—usually spiced with abundant references to hellfire and the consequences of failure to heed the Gospel message—those interested in joining the church were invited to come forward and be prayed over. People would go to the front of the tabernacle and kneel on the cold, dirty floor for as long as two hours while deacons and elders placed their palms on the candidates' foreheads, praying aloud for conversion.

Twice that fall, Fanny went to the altar. Twice she got down on her knees and the frenzied elders all but crushed her skull, laying hands upon her head and roaring prayers for her conversion. Twice the hours went by without her "getting happy."

Finally, on November 20, Fanny, now torn with frustration and anxiety, was led for a third time to the altar. This time she was frantic. "It seemed to me that the light must come then or never."

No other candidates presented themselves that night. For hours, the deacons and elders prayed, but nothing happened. The congregation began to sing Isaac Watts's consecration hymn, "Alas and Did My Saviour Bleed." At the fifth and last verse—"Here, Lord, I give myself away. 'Tis all that I can do."—it happened. Suddenly, Fanny felt "my very soul

SUDDENLY, FANNY FELT "MY VERY SOUL WAS FLOODED WITH CELESTIAL LIGHT."

was flooded with celestial light." She leaped to her feet, shouting, "Hallelujah! Hallelujah!" In her ecstasy, "for the first time I realized that I had been trying to hold the world in one hand and the Lord in the other."

It is difficult to review Fanny's life up to this time without having a distinct impression of Christian convictions from earliest childhood. However, something very significant did happen that night. If the experience were not the beginning of her Christian life, it certainly marked a pronounced deepening of it. It was perhaps what would be called by charismatics the "baptism of the Holy Spirit."

The "November Experience," as she called it, was a watershed in Fanny Crosby's life. Although there was no dramatic change in her life and she soon realized it did not solve all her spiritual problems, it marked the beginning of a deepening Christian experience and the beginning of total dedication to her life in God. Like most other young people, Fanny previously had lived in hopes of making a name for herself in the world, of making money, of attaining other earthly goals. Now, increasingly, she came to lay aside those ambitions.

The experience is frequently alluded to in many of her hymns and poems. It is in "At the Cross," written about 1900, and is described in more detail in the long, unpublished "Valley of Silence," written about two months before she died at the age of ninety-five:

I walk down the Valley of Silence,
Down the dim, voiceless valley alone,
And I hear not the fall of a footstep
Around me, save God's and my own;
And the hush of my heart is as holy
As hours when angels have flown.

Long ago I was weary of voices
Whose music my heart could not win,
Long ago I was weary of noises
That fretted my soul with their din;
Long ago I was weary with places,
When I met but the human and sin.
Do you ask what I found in this Valley?
'Tis my trysting place with the Divine,
For I fell at the feet of the Holy,
And above me a voice said, "Be Mine."
And there rose from the depth of my spirit,
The echo, "My heart shall be Thine."

She concluded:

Do you ask how I live in this Valley?
I weep and I dream and I pray;
But my tears are so sweet as the dewdrops
That fall from the roses in May,
And my prayer, like a perfume from censers,
Ascendeth to God night and day.

The "Valley of Silence," more than any of her writings, explains the mystical experience of November 20, 1850.

8
THE LYRICIST

In the early 1850s, the Institution was visited by such celebrities as the English poet Martin Farquhar Tupper; the "Swedish Nightingale," Jenny Lind; and Ole Bornemann Bull, the Norwegian violinist. When the famed soprano gave a concert of operatic arias, Swedish folk songs, and American patriotic airs, Fanny "could imagine that I was in heaven and hearing an angel sing." Fanny got to meet the blond, blue-eyed Lind personally at—of all unlikely places—a wake!

Fanny went to Bridgeport every summer and often brought friends with her. Mercy and the children, now living outside the city limits in the "Fairfield Woods," were enchanted by the visitors from the Great City. In manner, speech, and dress they seemed so very different from the rustic inhabitants of that rural community. Years later Fanny's older half-sister Julie would recall the fascination with which, as a tiny girl, she first sniffed the perfume Fanny brought on her visits.

Even though Mercy was a stern disciplinarian, she was also inquisitive and open-minded and never condemned her daughter for her perfume and jewelry. Mercy took an interest in the culture of the city and welcomed her daughter's guests, whether students or professors, eagerly following their conversation. She delighted them with her Puritan customs, New England cooking, and picturesque Yankee twang.

Jule and Carrie insisted that "every poem that I composed since I saw them before" be "duly recited and subjected to their criticism." Fortunately, these junior literary critics were unabashed admirers of their sister's work. Little Jule aspired to be a poet herself and imagined she could achieve her goal by creeping unobserved into her big sister's room at night, when Fanny was composing poetry, and copying exactly her physical gestures and position.

In the fall of 1853, a young man named William Cleveland was appointed head of the Institution's literary department. Shortly thereafter, he arranged the hiring of his sixteen-year-old brother, who was to teach reading, writing, arithmetic, and geography to the younger children and serve as a clerk in the office of the new superintendent, T. Colden Cooper. The boy's name was Grover.

Shortly after the Clevelands arrived, William consulted Fanny "in regard to the boy." Fanny, now the "preceptress," or dean of students, was recognized as the best-loved teacher on the faculty, a woman to whom both teachers and students went in times of difficulty. The Clevelands' father had died recently, William told her. "Grover has taken our father's death very much to heart, and I wish you would go into the office. . .and talk to him once in a while." Of course, Fanny agreed to do so.

The boy was quite mature for his age and, though very thin, was almost six feet tall and wore "a very respectable goatee." Young Cleveland was quiet and introverted. But Fanny was soon able to win his confidence, and he entered into a deep friendship with the older woman. Motherlike, Fanny took the young teacher under wing. She frequently warned him, when he seemed overly absorbed in bookish pursuits, not to "study too much and injure yourself."

Grover read to Fanny from his favorite poets, Lord Byron and Thomas Moore. He volunteered to copy down the poems she dictated. This collaboration on the job irritated Superintendent Cooper, and he began to give them a difficult time. In her writings, Fanny never referred to Cooper by name, but simply as a "cruel incompetent." She felt Cleveland's copying poems for her violated no rule.

On two occasions, Cooper stormed into Grover's office while the youth was copying poems dictated by Fanny. "Miss Crosby!" he snapped. "When you want Mr. Cleveland to copy a piece for you, I will thank you to ask me. My clerks have other work to do than copy poetry!" When she repeated the "offense," he forbade Fanny to even speak to Cleveland again without his permission.

Fanny seethed in silence. Her young colleague stepped in to give a few words of advice. "Now, Fanny Crosby, how long do you intend to allow that man to harrow up your feelings like that?" he asked soothingly.

"But what can I do to stop it?"

"By giving as good as he sent it!" said Cleveland. "Give him a few paragraphs of plain prose that he will not very soon forget."

"But Grover, I've never been saucy in my life," she protested.

"But it is not impudent to take your own part, and you never will be taught independence and self-reliance any younger," said the youth, lecturing the middle-aged teacher and dean as if she were his daughter.

To be lectured like a child by a boy half her age might have been nearly as offensive to her as Cooper's insolence, but she accepted Grover's counsel. The next day she was dictating to Grover when Cooper again flew into the office, this time exploding with curses, insults, and threats. Fanny turned and said icily, "I want you to understand that I am second to no one in this Institution except yourself, and I have borne with your insolence so long that I will do so no longer. If it is repeated, I will report you to the managers."

Cooper slunk from the office and gave her no more trouble.

The Clevelands hated the Institution. They found the building hideously ugly and the life there depressing. During Cooper's regime, the Institution became overcrowded, growing from about 60 students in 1850 to 116 three years

> **THE CHILDREN WERE TREATED MORE AS INMATES THAN PUPILS.**

later. The children were treated more as inmates than pupils. Cooper instituted severe punishments for minor offenses, whippings for major ones. The Cleveland brothers resigned in late 1854.

About the same time she met Grover Cleveland, Fanny came to work with a man who, though less important to American history, was to be far more important to her own future. She had known George Frederick Root for ten years. An American born the same year as she, he had studied in Europe and, on his return, worked diligently—as Lowell Mason had done—to introduce European-style music to America. He went so far (as did many musicians and artists of the day) as to Europeanize his name to George Friedrich Wurzel. Like many cultured people of the day, he considered American music crude and employed elements of the music of Handel, Haydn, Mozart, Beethoven, and others to write suave and sophisticated popular songs.

Root had given music lessons at the Institution in the 1840s, but it wasn't until the next decade that Fanny came to know him as a person. One day in 1851, Root was playing the piano, and Fanny was listening. The poet was deeply moved by the strains of an original composition, which sounded like the music of some

European master. "Oh, why don't you publish that, Mr. Root?" she asked.

Root, a small, bearded man, looked at her with his piercing, birdlike eyes and said, "Why, I have no words for it."

"Oh, I can think of words. Your melody says:

'O come to the greenwood, where nature is smiling,
Come to the greenwood, so lovely and gay,
There will soft music, thy spirit beguiling,
Tenderly carol thy sadness away.' "

Root was enthusiastic. "I can use you!" he said. "I need someone to supply words to the songs that I write. Would you be willing to do that?"

Fanny was too busy to work with him until the next summer, when she was offering courses at the Normal Academy of Music at North Reading, Massachusetts. Root, along with Lowell Mason, was a director, and it was here that Fanny began to supply words for his tunes.

Fanny wrote several songs that first summer. Root supplied all the music, Fanny all the words. At least two pieces became fairly popular: "Fare Thee Well, Kitty Dear" and "The Hazel Dell"—trite, tearfully sentimental songs of the type that appealed so much to listeners of that era. Root was pleased, recognizing Fanny as "a lady. . . who had a great gift for rhyming, and better still. . .a delicate and poetic imagination."

That autumn he put her to work on an absurd composition called "The Flower Queen," which Fanny later called "the first American cantata." Root, who already had the preposterous plot in mind, would tell her what he wanted certain characters to say, "and the next day the poem would be ready."

In fact, she sometimes had two or three poems ready. Root generally "hummed enough of the melody to give her an idea of the metre and rhythmic swing wanted, and sometimes played to her the entire music of a number" before she undertook the writing. He rarely saw fit to modify her poems and had only to choose between the alternate versions she had written. Root then "thought out the music" in its final form while commuting to classes.

"The Flower Queen" became popular all over the East Coast. The next summer, the two tried a similar composition, "The Pilgrim Fathers"—this time with Lowell Mason collaborating with Root in writing the melody to Fanny's poems. Later, Fanny collaborated with Root and William B. Bradbury in turning out another cantata.

> "THE FLOWER QUEEN" BECAME POPULAR ALL OVER THE EAST COAST.

During the summer of 1855, Fanny once again collaborated with Root in writing songs. Several became hits, including the slave song "They Have Sold Me Down the River," the morbid "Proud World, Goodbye," "Birth of the North," and "O, How Glad to Get Home." Three songs they wrote that year became especially popular: "The Honeysuckle Glen," about the death of a beautiful maiden; "Rosalie, the Prairie Flower," which became more popular than anything Fanny had written up to that time; and "There's Music in the Air," which was sung in schools and colleges well into the twentieth century.

Nobody knew Fanny Crosby was the lyricist for these songs, which appeared solely under Root's byline. The royalty on "Rosalie" amounted to three thousand dollars, but Fanny received only a dollar or two! Root bought the poems from Fanny, published them himself, and reaped the benefits of their popularity alone. He considered that he had no further obligation to Fanny after paying the standard fee publishing companies normally paid their poets.

While writing hit songs for Root, Fanny became reacquainted with a man who was to prove even more important in her life: her future husband. "Some people," she commented later, "seem to forget that blind girls have just as great a faculty for loving and do love just as much and just as truly as those who have their sight."

At thirty-five, Fanny "had a heart that was hungry for love," but she was still a spinster. Her increasing output of poems on disappointed love perhaps betrayed her frustration. However, in 1855, the Institution acquired a new teacher, Alexander Van Alstine, whom Fanny had met as a boy years earlier during a tour at Oswego, New York. "Van" studied for a few years at the Institution and became a brilliant pupil; in 1848, he became the first pupil from the Institution to enroll at a regular college. His chosen vocation was music; he also mastered Greek, Latin, philosophy, and theology. By the early 1850s, he had a teaching certificate and was giving music lessons in the Albion, New York, public schools. In 1855, he returned to the Institution as a music instructor.

At first, Fan and Van had merely a platonic relationship, based on their mutual love of music and poetry. Van became deeply interested in Fanny's poetry, and she became interested in his music. In her words, "Thus, we soon grew to be very much concerned for each other."

> VAN BECAME DEEPLY INTERESTED IN FANNY'S POETRY, AND SHE BECAME INTERESTED IN HIS MUSIC.

In the fall of 1857, Van left the Institution and began to give private music lessons in Maspeth, Long Island, in what is now the borough of Queens. Fanny was prepared to follow him. The "cruel incompetence" of Colden Cooper had made the Institution, once her "happy home," into a dreary place. Children were mistreated, teachers were underpaid, the building was ice cold in winter, and the meals grew increasingly bad. Devoted teachers like Van and Fanny felt they no longer could function well under Cooper's Spartan regime.

Fanny terminated her long relationship with the Institution March 2, 1858, and headed toward Long Island, marriage, and an independent life. They were married in a private ceremony March 5 in the little town of Maspeth. Van was twenty-seven, Fanny thirty-eight.

Her existence was changed altogether. She was no longer the center of attention, as she had been at the Institution, visited and feted by dignitaries. She no longer lived near the nation's greatest cultural center, famed as "the Blind Poetess." She was now a housewife, married to a struggling music teacher, living in rented rooms in a country town where few of the farmers, merchants, and laborers realized their blind, dwarflike neighbor was a nationally known poet.

Yet this life pleased her, for she never liked publicity and the attendant crowds. For the first time in two decades, she was back where she loved to be, in the country, and she felt she was living to benefit not so much the general public but her husband. In the spring of 1858, Fanny seemed to be on the threshold of a dream come true.

About her married life we know almost nothing. Precious little is known of her husband. We do not even know how his name was properly spelled; records show it as "Van Alstine" and "Van Alsteine," while in later life Fanny always spelled her married name (which she used only on legal documents) "Van Alstyne." In one of her autobiographies, Fanny says his father, an engineer, was "from the banks of the Rhine" and emigrated to the States as a young man. His mother was born in England. Van is said to have lost his sight in early childhood as a result of sickness. The two pictures we have of him indicate a handsome man, slender, with a finely chiseled Teutonic face, clean-shaven (unlike most men of his generation).

Van was one of New York's finest organ virtuosos. He also was proficient at piano, cornet, and other instruments. When he was at the keyboard, his features were said to be transformed into a look of unutterable delight. He was jovial and easy-going, apparently well liked. His mission in life was to make his beloved European classical masters available to the common people, and he concentrated on providing music lessons to poor children at low cost. To support Fanny and himself, he served as paid organist in various area churches.

In the late spring and early summer of 1858, Fanny was busy compiling a third volume of poetry, *A Wreath of Columbia's Flowers*. While there are many excellent poems in the collection, others are trite. Fanny included three short stories. There were poems on various subjects, ranging from the Metropolitan Police Force to unrequited love to the death of Daniel Webster. *A Wreath of Columbia's Flowers* was the least successful of her volumes of verse.

Meanwhile, there were changes in her family circle. Her uncle Joseph, with his wife and children, Frank and Ida, had gone to Savannah, Georgia, to open a regional branch of Crosby and May Saddle Goods. There he contracted tuberculosis and died May 2. The same year, Fanny's sister Jule married Byron Athington of Bridgeport. Jule was no longer the mischievous little sprite who disturbed her sister's attempt to write verse, but a plump, dark-haired young woman, short but still a head taller than her older sister. Mercy continued to live at Fairfield Woods with fourteen-year-old Carrie.

About 1859, Fanny became a mother, but the child died in

infancy. This was perhaps the greatest misfortune of Fanny's life. She almost never spoke of it. We do not know whether the baby was a girl or boy or the cause of death.

> ABOUT 1859, FANNY BECAME A MOTHER, BUT THE CHILD DIED IN INFANCY.

After this tragedy, Fanny's dream of a quiet, secluded life on rural Long Island seemed to have been exploded. She gradually recovered, but she longed to return to familiar surroundings. What was once a rustic paradise had become an inferno, and she yearned to escape the scenes of her suffering. So she and Van returned to Manhattan about 1860 and took a room a few blocks from the Institution.

The New York City to which they returned was a city engulfed in the zeal of religious revival.

9
THE SECOND GREAT AWAKENING

The revival began before Fanny left the Institution and grew to tremendous proportions during her stay in Maspeth. There had been two or three previous revivals in American history, starting with the First Great Awakening in the 1740s. Now, on the heels of an economic depression, there was again an intensified interest in religion. A full-scale revival, sometimes called the Second Great Awakening, swept the nation.

Apart from the workings of the Holy Spirit, certain human factors tended to foster the revival. One was the growth of Sunday schools. "Sunday school" originally was the name for the nineteenth-century equivalent of today's night school, in which working people could pursue a secular education by attending classes on their only day off work. Soon, religious education—especially for the young—became popular on Sunday, too.

A second factor was the growth of mission societies. These were not only for the propagation of religion but also for the abolition of such evils as slavery, liquor, and tobacco and the amelioration of other social ills. During the 1840s and '50s, there was a great growth in home mission societies dedicated to spreading the Gospel of Jesus Christ among the increasingly large numbers of unchurched in the nation's rapidly growing towns and cities.

The most significant of these groups was the Young Men's Christian Association. Introduced in England, the YMCA appeared in America in the early 1850s. Its goals were to promote "evangelical religion," cultivate the living of the Christian life, and improve "the mental and spiritual condition of young men." The YMCA provided devotional meetings and classes for Bible instruction, as well as mission and Sunday schools. It engaged in social action, organizing community relief activities to help the needy and oppressed. Libraries and reading rooms were set up, and lectures were held "to amuse, interest and instruct." To spread the Gospel, the YMCA sent young men to preach on street corners and wharves, in fire houses, and sometimes in tents.

It was in this capacity that the career of D. L. Moody, with whom Fanny Crosby's name would become inextricably linked, had its beginnings, on the north side of Chicago. Moody achieved great success in bringing boys from the slums to participate in the Y's programs and, through the activities and fellowship provided by that organization, to become successful and respected Christian citizens. In New York, too, the YMCA was active. Here, the guiding light was Dr. Howard Crosby (1824–1891), a distant cousin of Fanny's. The young pastor of the Fourth Avenue Presbyterian Church was a charter member of the New York YMCA and its second president. He considered the YMCA an "extension of the church" and labored to spread its work among New York's seven hundred thousand inhabitants.

Revivals began to occur in the Great City and other parts of the country in 1857. Prayer meetings sprang up all over the New York area, and conversions were professed daily. So great and widespread were the revivals that newspapers gave them extensive daily coverage. Between 1858 and 1860, it was claimed that fifty thousand conversions occurred each week in the nation, and that each week some ten thousand were united with a church for the first time.

Christians went from door to door, witnessing in dingy attics and squalid cellars as well as in elegant parlors and opulent drawing rooms. They invited their hosts to attend Sunday school and inquirers' classes. And they came in droves! As many as twelve hundred people a day packed the John Street Methodist Church for noonday prayer meetings.

Fanny's life was much affected by the revivals. She began attending the John Street church, where she became active in the sewing societies, knitting garments for the poor. She attended prayer meetings there and at Henry Ward Beecher's Plymouth Congregational Church, getting to know the celebrated pulpit orator, whom she soon came to count as a friend.

FANNY'S LIFE WAS MUCH AFFECTED BY THE REVIVALS.

In the midst of the revival, the Civil War broke out. Every man in the Bridgeport area where Fanny's relatives lived was drafted or enlisted. Byron Athington, her brother-in-law, at twenty-four gave up a promising business to answer his country's call. Fanny's "brother," as she called her mother's stepson, William Morris, also enlisted.

Fanny was very proud of her relatives. Formerly a Democrat, then a Whig, she now was an ardent Republican and would remain so the rest of her life. Quite a jingoist, she always had carried a miniature silk flag, but now she took to pinning it to her blouse.

Her fanatical ardor for the Union almost led her to fighting. Fanny was eating at a Manhattan restaurant one evening when a southern lady was irritated to the point of hysteria by Fanny's flaunting of the Union emblem. "Take that dirty thing away!" the woman snapped when she saw the flag.

Fanny, to the astonishment of her companions, flew into a towering rage, sprang from her chair, and rushed in the direction of the voice. "Repeat that remark at your risk!" she threatened.

The restaurant manager, attracted by the shrill cries, came onto the scene just in time to prevent blows.

Back in Bridgeport, Fanny's sister Carrie wed a man named Lee Barnum, and Mercy went to live with the newlyweds in an apartment on Grand Street. The war was not kind to the Morris clan. William contracted tuberculosis. It did not kill him for nearly two decades, but upon his return, he passed it on to his son Walter. Athington was severely wounded in Virginia in 1863 and would never fully recover.

These events intensified Fanny's patriotism. During the war, she wrote patriotic songs that were set to music by Dan Emmett and other musicians. They are of blood-curdling bellicosity. In "Union Song," she wrote:

> *Death to those whose impious hands*
> *Burst our Union's sacred bands,*
> *Vengeance thunders, right demands—*
> *Justice for the brave.*

In "Song to Jeff Davis," she urged menacingly:

> *Come, thou vaunting boaster,*
> *Jeff Davis and thy clan,*
> *Our northern troops are waiting,*
> *Now, show thyself a man.*

Advance with all thy forces,
We dare thy traitor band,
We'll blow thy ranks to atoms!
We'll fight them hand to hand!

Now, Jeff, when thou art needy,
Lead on thy rebel crew,
We'll give them all a welcome—
With balls and powder too!
We spurn thy constitution!
We spurn thy southern laws!
Our stars and stripes are waving,
And Heav'n will speed our cause.

The song ends with a threat to decapitate the southern leader.

These lines are truly remarkable, coming from the pen of a woman whose work is distinguished by sentiment and sensitivity—even saccharine sweetness. Most of the popular songs of that period were distinguished for their emotional intensity and sentimental nature, relating the war to a personal situation. Fanny's Civil War songs were savage rallying cries, devoid of warmth or human interest.

When the war was not on her mind, however, she retained her touch. And in the midst of the war she was given the opportunity to use her gift of writing verse in a way that would bring far more recognition than her secular poetry, her musicianship, or her work as a teacher had ever accomplished.

She always had been eclectic in her church going, and at forty-three she was not a member of any church. Partial for years to Methodism, she frequently attended the John Street church. In addition, she often went to the Plymouth Congregational Church in Brooklyn to hear her friend Beecher, who was her favorite preacher; the Fifth Avenue Presbyterian Church, whose pastor was Dr. John Hall; the Fourth Avenue Presbyterian Church of her cousin Howard Crosby; and Trinity Episcopal Church.

She also attended the Dutch Reformed Church on Twenty-third Street. The pastor, Rev. Peter Stryker, was delighted to make the acquaintance of "the Blind Poetess" and thrilled when she responded to his request to write a New Year's Eve hymn. Knowing of her depression at the loss of her child, Stryker told her his friend William Bradbury needed someone to provide lyrics for his melodies. He recommended that she see Bradbury at once, and Fanny agreed to go.

The Second Great Awakening brought about great changes in American hymnody. The need was felt for a type of hymn that would match the new approach in presenting Christian doctrine. Lowell Mason, considered the father of American church music, long before had set forth his "canons," and these instructions on the aim and nature of hymnody, published in his widely circulated *Church Psalmody* in 1831, were still

THE SECOND GREAT AWAKENING BROUGHT ABOUT GREAT CHANGES IN AMERICAN HYMNODY.

definitive for American hymn writing. "The sentiments and imagery," he wrote, "should be grave, dignified." Also, "Whatever is unscriptural, groveling. . .light, [or] fanciful. . . should be avoided," because it tended to "check the flow of the soul." Moreover, "familiar and fondling epithets or forms of expression, applied to either person of the Godhead, should be avoided, as bringing with them associations highly unfavorable to pure devotional feeling."

Mason called for heavy emphasis on sin and hell. He disparaged any hymn that tended to make the worshippers "feel good," for all emphasis should be on the sinner's need for repentance.

These stern hymns now were falling out of favor. The "revived" of the 1850s and '60s wanted hymns that were personal, light, and informal. A few of those written in the past fit this description and were well used, such as "My Faith Looks Up to Thee" by Ray Palmer; "Nearer, My God, to Thee" by Sarah Flower Adams; "Just as I Am, Without One Plea" by Charlotte Elliott; "Abide with Me" by Rev. Francis Lyte; Charles Wesley's "Jesus, Lover of My Soul"; and A.M. Toplady's "Rock of Ages."

Some musicians were answering the call. George Root had turned to Sunday school music. Another composer of Sunday school hymns was the Baptist minister Robert Lowry, who in 1864 wrote the all-time hit "Shall We Gather at the River?" The most important and prolific hymn writer of the period was Bradbury, who had collaborated with Root and Fanny in the cantata "Daniel." Born in Maine in 1816, Bradbury had studied music under Lowell Mason. Early in his career, he helped introduce the organ to American churchgoers.

While a young man, Bradbury was appointed organist at New York's Baptist Tabernacle and started singing classes there. For many years at the tabernacle he held an annual Juvenile Musical Festival—one of the biggest musical events in the city. At thirty, Bradbury had gone to England and Germany to study composition. Returning to New York, he began to manufacture Bradbury pianos and compose songs and other musical works. Like Root's, his melodies applied much of the European masters' style to American music and often were adaptations of melodies by Beethoven, Handel, and other major composers. Bradbury's songs were distinguished by their "easy, natural flow," his harmonies by their simplicity.

Some complained Bradbury was neither performer nor composer. Others claimed he was ruining American music with his melodies imitating European composers. But he endeared himself to many of the faithful with his musical settings of "Just as I Am," "He Leadeth Me," "Saviour, Like a Shepherd, Lead Us" and "On Christ, the Solid Rock, I Stand." The tunes may have been sneered at by highbrow critics, but they were loved by the masses.

Not only did Bradbury want to provide light, melodic settings for existing hymns, he also wanted to set newly written poems to music. He was dissatisfied with the quality of verse submitted to him. So he was overjoyed when Stryker informed him, in January 1864, that he shortly would be meeting a lady who probably would be the answer to his problems.

Fanny, too, was enthusiastic. She felt God had given her a new reason for existing; she was convinced He wanted to use her talents in writing hymns.

Fanny met Bradbury February 2 at the Ponton Hotel on Broome Street. He was a very thin man with

FANNY FELT GOD WANTED TO USE HER TALENTS IN WRITING HYMNS.

a pinched face, framed by a lionlike mane of thick, bushy dark hair and a gigantic beard. Fanny could not see his face, but she could perceive his character. Not only was she subject to visions and trances; she also had that strange faculty of reading a person's character from the emanating "overtones." She liked Bradbury even as he liked her, and he immediately put their relationship on a first-name basis.

"Fanny," he said, "I thank God that we have at last met, for I think you can write hymns, and I have wished for a long time to have a talk with you."

Bradbury introduced Fanny to his assistant, her old friend from Ridgefield, Sylvester Main. Sylvester had come to New York many years before to open a music school. He was now a pillar of the Norfolk Street Methodist Church and a well-known soloist in New York churches.

Fanny agreed to return within a week with a hymn by which Bradbury could sample her abilities. "It now seemed to me that the great work of my life had really begun." Three days later, she was back with a three-stanza poem that began:

We are going, we are going
To a home beyond the skies,
Where the fields are robed in beauty
And the sunlight never dies.
Where the fount of joy is flowing
In the valley green and fair,
We shall dwell in love together,
There shall be no parting there.

The hymn was everything Bradbury had been looking for. Light and informal in verse, it was reasonably good poetry and contained great warmth and emotional power. He decided to use "We Are Going" in the hymnal he was preparing.

The next week, Bradbury sent for Fanny in haste, saying he needed a war song (he also published secular music). He suggested, as the first line, "There's a sound among the mulberry trees." Fanny changed it to "There's a sound among the forest trees." Bradbury then played the melody for which she was to write the words. It was difficult, but after hearing it two or three times, she was able to count the measure and find suitable words.

Bradbury was incredulous. He had given her a cruelly difficult melody to test her, never imagining she could put words to the music. But she had passed the test with flying colors!

"Fanny," he said, "I'm surprised! And while I have a publishing house, you will always have work."

> "FANNY, WHILE I HAVE A PUBLISHING HOUSE, YOU WILL ALWAYS HAVE WORK."

And so Fanny went to work for the firm of William B. Bradbury and Company.

10
WRITING HYMNS

Fanny joined Mary Ann Kidder and Josephine Pollard in a "trio" to produce the bulk of the poems Bradbury and his colleagues set to music for Sunday school hymn books. The first Bradbury hymnal to which Fanny contributed was *The Golden Censer* (1864). "We Are Going," which was given the title "Our Bright Home Above," and "There's a Cry from Macedonia" were credited to Fanny. She may have contributed other hymns, but Bradbury, following the practice of Root and other publishers, did not always designate the authors.

Other hymnals followed.

Most of her hymns would appear under the name of "Miss Fanny J. Crosby." When they married, Van realized his middle-aged bride had a career and reputation of her own, and he felt that to have her change her name was subordinating her career to his. So he encouraged her to maintain her own career and name. Fanny variously called herself "Miss Crosby," "Mrs. Crosby," and "Madam Crosby." Whenever she had to write her married name, for legal reasons, she used "Van Alstyne."

> FANNY VARIOUSLY CALLED HERSELF "MISS CROSBY," "MRS. CROSBY," AND "MADAM CROSBY."

The Civil War was over, but Fanny's work as a hymn writer

was just beginning. Bradbury was preparing another hymnal, and Fanny was asked to supply hymns. Usually, the music came first. Bradbury would give Fanny a tune for which she was to provide the words; often, he would give her the title and subject, too. This was not always the case, however, and frequently she was allowed to choose the topic, often providing the poem before Bradbury or one of his colleagues wrote the music.

Sometimes Fanny's poems were inspired by trivial bits of conversation—as, for instance, the afternoon she, Bradbury, Vet Main, and an eminent musician named Philip Phillips were "discussing various things" and Phillips looked at his watch and realized he had to go. "Good night," he said, "until we meet in the morning."

When he had left, Fanny turned to Bradbury and remarked, "If I write a hymn for that subject, will you compose the music?" The composer agreed, and Fanny wrote a funeral hymn:

> *Goodnight! Goodnight!*
> *'Till we meet in the morning,*
> *Far above this fleeting shore;*
> *To endless joy in a moment awaking,*
> *There we'll sleep no more.*

Robert Lowry, author of "Shall We Gather at the River?", set the poem to music.

Bradbury was a sick man when he and Fanny first met, and he told her from the start he knew he had but a short time to live. In April 1866 he was so ill he had to go South in hopes of regaining his health. He remained there all summer.

Meanwhile, Fanny was not idle. She reported regularly to the office to prepare poems and receive melodies for the new volume.

Her talents had come to the attention of other writers and publishers of church music. One of them was Phoebe Palmer Knapp, who became one of Fanny's most devoted friends. Born about 1835, Phoebe was married to Joseph Fairchild Knapp, who later founded the Metropolitan Life Insurance Company. Her understanding of Christianity was to aid the poor and foster social reform.

Phoebe was attractive, tall and slim, with fine, regular features, intense eyes, and dark, curling hair. Although deeply concerned about the plight of the poor, she by no means disdained the life of the rich. She was a lavish dresser, given to wearing elaborate gowns and diamond tiaras. The "Knapp Mansion," a palatial residence in Brooklyn, was a New York institution where she held a European-style salon, entertaining most of the prominent people of the day. Almost every Republican president, Union general, and Methodist bishop was entertained there.

Her evening musicales were the talk of the town. In her music room was one of the finest collections of musical instruments in the country, and many well-known artists and performers were her guests.

Very talkative, Phoebe had the reputation of a smothering, possessive, strong-willed woman and a bizarre eccentric. She considered herself a better musician than she actually was.

Nevertheless, Fanny came to love Phoebe and was a frequent guest at the Knapp Mansion, where she enjoyed free access to the music room. At the mansion, she was introduced to such dignitaries as Presidents

SHE WAS INTRODUCED TO SUCH DIGNITARIES AS PRESIDENTS GRANT, HAYES, GARFIELD, MCKINLEY, AND TEDDY ROOSEVELT.

Grant, Hayes, Garfield, McKinley, and Teddy Roosevelt. Here, she frequently conversed with her friend Henry Ward Beecher and his sister, Harriet Beecher Stowe. She came to know the bloody general, William Tecumseh Sherman, the temperance crusader, Frances Willard, and the poet, Alice Cary.

Phoebe would have done more for Fanny, who was living in poverty, but the poet refused her beneficence. She provided Phoebe with many poems, which Phoebe set to music and published through a brother who owned a publishing company.

Another musician who became seriously interested in Fanny's talents was Philip Phillips. He was fourteen years younger than Fanny but had gained nationwide renown through his song services. His beautiful baritone renditions of hymns had considerable influence on listeners.

Phillips occasionally called upon Fanny to provide him with a hymn or two for his evangelistic services. In 1866, he was busy preparing a hymnal to be titled *The Singing Pilgrim, or Pilgrim's Progress, Illustrated in Song for the Sabbath School and Family.* It was centered around John Bunyan's seventeenth-century classic. He asked Fanny to write hymns based on the thought contained in various selections of the book; he himself would provide the tunes.

He gave her a selection of seventy-five quotations of a few lines each. Fanny memorized them and selected forty she thought appropriate for hymns. Then she composed forty poems in her head. When the last one had been completed, she dictated them one after the other to her secretary at Bradbury's office.

Phillips and everyone else was amazed at Fanny's phenomenal memory, but she made light of it, saying every person without sight has to develop the memory—and others could do it, too, if they were unable to refer to the written word.

Her forty hymns comprised the bulk of *The Singing Pilgrim*, which became very popular and was circulated widely. But few people knew who wrote the popular lyrics, for Phillips, like Root, paid Fanny a dollar or two for her efforts and then published the hymns under his own name.

In addition to visiting Phoebe Knapp, Fanny spent a great deal of time with her neighbors in the tenements where she and Van boarded in Manhattan. She staged her own soirées in the dingy houses, gathering residents for an evening of song, accompanied by guitar.

She and her husband seem to have gone their separate ways. Van had his circle of friends and activities, Fanny had hers, and they seemed content that way. Each retained a lively interest in the other's career without really becoming a part of it.

Bradbury returned from the South in the fall of 1866, apparently improved in health. The following year, *Fresh Laurels* was published. In addition to the title hymn, it contained eleven hymns attributed to Fanny Crosby or one of her pen names. Of varying quality, they showed simplicity, directness, emotional power, and a relationship to daily life—earmarks of her art.

In 1867, Fanny and Van were living on Varick Street on the Lower West Side, in half of a third-floor garret. This tenement, where thirty-three people were crowded into an unbelievably small space, was far from the worst of New York's slums. All the neighbors seem to have been respectable, working-class people. There were dressmakers, gold beaters, hackmen, carriage painters, truckmen, and grocery clerks. Ethnically, there were many Irish, Germans, and blacks; Fanny and Van were among the minority of white Anglo-Saxons.

There was no outside ventilation or running water in the rooms.

Fanny and Van could have lived in better circumstances, but Fanny insisted on giving away all she received that was not required for their basic needs. She wanted to live with the poor as one of them, for she believed part of her mission in life was to them. These people saw the good things in life passing them by, going to others. It was for them she wrote hymns like the following:

> **FANNY INSISTED ON GIVING AWAY ALL SHE RECEIVED THAT WAS NOT REQUIRED FOR BASIC NEEDS.**

> *Pass me not, O gentle Saviour,*
> *Hear my humble cry;*
> *While on others Thou art smiling,*
> *Do not pass me by.*

She wrote for the wretched souls who "seemed drunk half the time" and had to sleep on the rooftops in summer because of the stifling heat, those at the bottom of the social ladder, whose dwellings were unspeakably filthy and falling apart, who collected rags, bones, and driblets of coal that fell from passing wagons.

She also wrote verses for the wealthy, urging social activism:

> *When, cheerful, we meet in our pleasant home,*
> *And the song of joy is swelling,*
> *Do we pause to think of the tears that flow*
> *In sorrow's lonely dwelling?*

Many have supposed the extreme simplicity of most of her hymns represented the depth of her intellect. This was not true. Her goal was not to compose poetry that would be admired by college professors and literary critics, but would be understood by common people.

She felt the same way about music. She apparently knew and loved Italian opera and was an excellent soprano, organist, pianist, and harpist. She knew well the compositions of Beethoven, Chopin, and Mendelssohn. But she also knew most people did not comprehend this music. The congregational hymn was for the untrained singer; music was something in which every worshipper should be able to participate. For her, the best poetry for the congregational hymn was pop verse, and the best music was the pop tune.

In November 1867, after completing the libretto for an oratorio by Philip Phillips called *Triumph of the Cross*, Fanny met a man who would become her most frequent collaborator and the composer of tunes to her most successful hymns. William Howard Doane was a wealthy Cincinnati manufacturer. Born in Connecticut in 1832, he began his business career at sixteen in his father's cotton goods firm and rapidly rose to success.

Doane had a second career. From early childhood, he was precocious in the field of music. At sixteen, he wrote a song called "The Grave Beneath the Willows." Throughout his early years in business, he directed church choirs and led various musical societies. He had a good voice and had become rather well known as a church soloist while living in Cincinnati.

Music was only a hobby for him until he was thirty, when he nearly died of a heart attack. A devout Baptist, Doane interpreted his illness as God's chastening. He decided God wanted him to devote more time to writing sacred melodies. Almost immediately after his recovery, he compiled a book of hymns called *Sabbath School Gems*, followed by *The Sunbeam* in 1864, and *The Silver Spray* (coedited with Theodore Perkins) in 1867.

Doane was dissatisfied with his hymns, believing they lacked suitable words. Like Bradbury, he tried for a while to write his own lyrics, but he was no poet, and the lyricists he engaged were no better.

That November, while in New York, he visited a friend, Rev. Dr. W. C. Van Meter, who directed what was known as the Five Points Mission. Van Meter knew Doane wrote hymn tunes and asked him for a melody to use on the anniversary of the founding of his mission. Doane replied that the melody would be no problem, but did Van Meter have words? Van Meter gave him a poem he thought might be suitable.

Doane did not like it and searched through his briefcase in vain for something better. Then, kneeling on the floor of his hotel room in prayer, he asked God to send him a poem for the celebration. He also asked God, as he had asked Him many times before, to send him a poet who could supply religious verse suitable for music.

At once, he heard a knock on the door. Opening it, he saw a little boy with an envelope addressed to him. The letter read: *Mr. Doane: I have never met you, but I feel impelled to send you this hymn. May God bless it.* It was signed, *Fanny Crosby.* Accompanying the note was a poem that began as follows:

More like Jesus would I be,
Let my Saviour dwell with me,
Fill my soul with peace and love,
Make me gentle as the dove;
More like Jesus as I go,
Pilgrim, in this world below;
Poor in spirit would I be—
Let my Saviour dwell in me.

THE WORDS SEEMED VERITABLY TO SING THEMSELVES TO HIM.

The words seemed veritably to sing themselves to him. What song could be more appropriate for the anniversary of a home mission than one that appealed to God for the grace to be "more like Jesus"?

Doane had no trouble writing a gentle, easy tune for these words. He once again prayed, giving thanks to the Almighty for sending him not only the poem but his long-sought poet.

At a neighboring church the next day, Van Meter pumped the organ while Doane played and sang the hymn. Van Meter burst into tears, so emotionally affected he had to stop pumping. He came from behind the organ, his eyes shining, and threw both arms around Doane's neck, crying, "Oh, Doane, where did you get that poem?"

Doane told him and inquired about the author. Van Meter gave him Fanny's address. Doane had too many commitments to call on her during that trip, but he resolved to do so the next time he was in New York.

Bradbury was slowly and painfully dying of consumption. Because of his illness and his inability to set her poems to music anymore, Fanny had been urged by Bradbury's friend, Robert Lowry, to send her latest poem to Doane.

In his farewell talk with her, Bradbury instructed Fanny to "take up my life work where I lay it down." He wanted her to assume leadership in the Sunday school hymn movement when he was dead. Racked with excruciating pain, he died in January 1868 at fifty-one.

Fanny was heartbroken. At his funeral, in compliance with a request the composer had made shortly before he died, the choir sang the first hymn he and Fanny had written together: "We Are Going, We Are Going to a Home Beyond the Skies." Filing by the casket, Fanny broke down in tears. It was then that she heard a mysterious voice, "clear and beautiful," that said to her, "Fanny, pick up the work where Bradbury has left it. Take your harp from the willow, and dry your tears."

Several others heard the voice but could not determine its source.

11
SAFE IN THE ARMS OF JESUS

After Bradbury's death, the publishing company was reorganized by his colleague Sylvester Main and a local merchant named Lucius Horatio Biglow (1833–c.1910). Although Vet Main occasionally wrote music, he and Biglow were primarily businessmen, and they generally left the work of producing hymns to the poets and musicians associated with the firm. Of these, Fanny rapidly became the most prominent and in many ways was responsible more than anyone else for setting the style of the hymns the new company produced for the next half-century. She seldom wrote music, but she pronounced on the suitability of the numerous tunes submitted to her for lyrics.

Soon after Bradbury was buried, Howard Doane returned to New York and looked up Fanny. He was horrified at the dilapidated condition of the old Varick Street tenement and unnerved by the stares of the tenants of all colors, who gawked at the impeccably dressed gentleman with the fashionable Vandyke beard. Doane forced Fanny to accept reluctantly what she understood to be two dollars, the standard fee for the poem she had written. When he left, she discovered he had given her twenty dollars.

Thus began a collaboration that would last forty-seven years. Howard Doane and Fanny Crosby came to be close personal friends, and Fanny often spent her summers with him and his wife, who also was named Fanny, and their daughters, Ida and Marguerite.

Doane, who was to set more than a thousand of Fanny's hymns to music, was not a great musician. He was best at writing simple, straightforward, marchlike tunes. His melodies, distinguished for their catchiness, relied heavily on the tradition of such songs as "Hail to the Chief" and "Columbia, the Gem of the Ocean."

But Fanny liked to collaborate with Doane. She believed simple, catchy tunes were best understood and remembered by most people. One must remember that in those days there was little opportunity for people to hear a repeated melody, for there were no recordings, and most people were too poor to own a piano—or even a hymnal. So when one first heard the tune of a hymn, it often was a matter of memorizing it then or not at all.

> **FANNY BELIEVED SIMPLE, CATCHY TUNES WERE BEST UNDERSTOOD AND REMEMBERED.**

Doane was a rare breed: a Christian business tycoon. He apparently came by his fabulous wealth honestly and never was accused of greed, injustice, or corruption. He gave a large percent of his income to charitable institutions in a time before tax laws made it expedient for the rich to do so. He was an active lay worker in the Mount Auburn Baptist Church in the Cincinnati suburb where he had a mansion.

As a businessman, he patented seventy inventions and so perfected the productivity of woodworking machines that, in 1889, France named him a Chevalier in the famed Legion of Honor. As a musician, he composed twenty-three hundred hymns over a period of fifty-three years.

A few days after their first meeting, he returned one evening and asked if Fanny could write him a poem using the phrase, "Pass me not, O gentle Saviour." She said she would, but uninspired, she wrote nothing for several weeks. Then, in the early spring of 1868, she was speaking at religious services in a prison near Manhattan. During the course of the services, she heard an inmate cry out piteously, "Good Lord! Do not pass me by!"

When she retired that evening, she wrote these words:

Pass me not, O gentle Saviour,
Hear my humble cry,
While on others Thou art smiling,
Do not pass me by.

Saviour, Saviour,
Hear my humble cry,
While on others Thou art calling,
Do not pass me by.

She sent the words to Doane, who soon wrote a melody. The hymn was sung a few days later at the prison where Fanny had been inspired and where she was still holding services. It made a profound impression on the prisoners, some of whom were converted on the spot. Fanny was so moved by the prisoners' reaction that she fell in a swoon and had to be carried out.

On April 30, Doane again appeared at Fanny's flat. "I have exactly forty minutes," he said, "before I must meet a train for Cincinnati. I have a tune for you. See if it says anything to you. Perhaps you can commit it to memory and then compose a poem to match it." He hummed a simple, plaintive melody.

After hearing it but once, Fanny clapped her hands, as she did whenever something pleased her. "Why, that says, 'Safe in the arms of Jesus!' " She wrote her best hymns when the tunes "said" something to her.

Scurrying to the other room of her tiny apartment, she knelt on the floor, as was her custom before composing a hymn, and asked God for inspiration. Seeing that His servant was in a hurry, God saw fit to grant it quickly. Within a half-hour, Fanny had a complete poem. During that time,

> **FANNY WROTE HER BEST HYMNS WHEN THE TUNES "SAID" SOMETHING TO HER.**

she claimed she was "wholly unconscious" of her surroundings and of everything except the hymn, which formed itself in her mind with no exertion on her part. She always claimed that hymn was not her own doing but was entirely the work of the "Blessed Holy Spirit."

Returning to Doane, she quickly dictated:

Safe in the arms of Jesus,
Safe on His gentle breast,
There, by His love o'ershaded,
Sweetly my soul shall rest.
Hark! 'tis the voice of angels,
Borne in a song to me,
Over the fields of glory,
Over the jasper sea.

Safe in the arms of Jesus,
Safe on His gentle breast,
There, by His love o'ershaded,
Sweetly my soul shall rest....

It became an instant success. After Biglow and Main included it in a hymnal three years later, it was widely sung all over the country.

Fanny always had a special attachment to "Safe in the Arms of Jesus." She claimed she had written it "for dead relatives" and for mothers who had lost their children. Could it have been inspired by the memory of her dead child?

The following year, Doane invited Fanny to his home for the first of many visits. She addressed a group of working men in Cincinnati. Toward the end of her talk, she had an overwhelming sensation that "some mother's boy" in the audience "must be rescued that night or not at all." She pleaded urgently, "If there is a dear boy here tonight who has perchance wandered away from his mother's home and his mother's teaching, would you please come to me at the close of the service?"

Sure enough, a young man of about eighteen came to her and asked, "Did you mean me?" He told Fanny he had promised his mother he would meet her in heaven, "but the way I have been living, I don't think that will be possible now."

Fanny prayed earnestly over the youth, and "he finally arose with a new light in his eyes and exclaimed, 'Now I can meet my mother in heaven, for now I have found her God!'"

Doane recently had asked Fanny to write a hymn on the home missions theme "Rescue the Perishing." That night before she went to bed, she had composed a complete hymn, beginning as follows:

Rescue the perishing,
Care for the dying,
Snatch them in pity from sin and the grave;
Weep o'er the erring one,
Lift up the fallen,
Tell them of Jesus the mighty to save.

The next day she recited it to Doane, who immediately gave it a stirring tune. Published the next year in his *Songs of Devotion* (along with "Pass Me Not"), it became a virtual battle cry of home mission workers all over the country.

Biglow and Main of New York and the John Church Company of Cincinnati were among the nation's largest publishers of hymns. From the late 1860s, Fanny dominated the hymnals published by the New York firm, contributing between a third and a half of the selections. So prolific was her writing, the editors had to induce her to use pen names to disguise the fact that they depended so heavily on one lyricist. Besides signing her name as "Fannie," "F.A.N.," "F.J.C.," "Fanny Van Alstyne," "Mrs. Alexander Van Alstyne," and "Mrs. Van A.," she was using frankly weird appellations: "L.L.A.," "J.W.W.," "###," "*" and "The Children's Friend." In the 1880s and '90s, she expanded her list of pseudonyms to include "Carrie Hawthorne," "Louise W. Tilden," "Maud Marion," "Ryan A. Dykes," "H. N. Lincoln," and others.

The use of pseudonyms was common among her friends, too. Ira Sankey also used the name "Rian A. (or "Ryan A.") Dykes." George Coles Stebbins often wrote simply as "George Coles." Charles H. Gabriel, who was to set many of Fanny's poems to music in the early 1900s, had seventeen *noms de plume*. But none could match her fanciful collection of 204 pen names!

Fanny was in great demand by composers of hymns, and she had no trouble meeting the demands. In forty-seven years, she would furnish Biglow and Main alone with 5,959 hymns (although only

> FANNY WAS IN GREAT DEMAND BY COMPOSERS OF HYMNS, AND SHE HAD NO TROUBLE MEETING THE DEMANDS.

about 2,000 were published). When a subject was suggested, she often wrote several poems, allowing the composer to choose one.

Naturally, by writing so much, the quality of her verse suffered. But at the same time, she was producing some of her most popular songs.

Fanny continued to write for composers not officially working for Biglow and Main. Besides contributing heavily to Philip Phillips's *Musical Leaves* (1868), in 1869 she contributed more than twenty hymns to Phoebe Knapp, who compiled *Notes of Joy*. John Robson Sweney, a Philadelphia songwriter whom Fanny was yet to meet, published some of her hymns in his hymnals. By the early 1870s, she was well on her way to becoming the queen of hymn writers.

Fanny often matched her poems to familiar tunes. An example is "We Thank Thee, Our Father," written to the melody of the famous "Adeste Fidelis." She set poems to Scottish and Welsh airs and used tunes by Stephen Foster.

A first-rate classical musician, Fanny was eminently capable of writing her own music. Privately, she improvised on the piano; many of her compositions were said to be beautiful, but she refused to have them written down. She also wrote hymn tunes, few of which were published. She felt the tunes she liked to compose were too difficult for the common worshipper. She and Van compiled a hymnal of their own about this time. Biglow and Main rejected it because it was felt by the directors that the public did not care for hymnals with all the selections written by only two people. It's possible their hymns also were considered too difficult and sophisticated for the popular taste.

The only hymns ever published for which she supplied both music and words are "Jesus, Dear, I Come to Thee," "The Blood-Washed Throng" (included in her 1906 autobiography), and a spring carol.

The lyrical staff of Biglow and Main included William J. Stevenson, Josephine Pollard, and Kate Cameron. Perhaps the best known, besides Fanny, was Anna Bartlett Warner, who wrote the world's most popular hymn, "Jesus Loves Me." Fanny also worked with Mrs. Mary Ann Kidder, Annie Sherwood Hawks, Mrs. Elizabeth Payson Prentiss, and the aging invalid, Lydia Baxter.

One of the most prominent writers of music for her words was Robert Lowry. By far their most successful collaboration was "All the Way My Saviour Leads Me," published in 1875. Six years younger than Fanny, Lowry was a distinguished Baptist minister who could thrill audiences with his extraordinary descriptive talent, but music was his first love. Lowry always said he could reach more people through hymns than through sermons.

Lowry's skill as a composer was almost as limited as Doane's and other contemporaries'. He was best with hymns that called for a martial, brass-band style, like "Shall We Gather at the River?" A pleasant, jolly, bearded man known as the "Good Doctor," he was an intellectual. Fanny loved to have him read poetry to her. He was sensitive to musical quality, and it rankled him that he could succeed only in the genre of what he termed "brass-band music."

Fanny wrote almost no hymns for Sylvester Main, a kind, gentle man whom she knew as a "faithful counselor and guide." He was more involved in the business of the firm than in composing. But Vet's son Hugh, then an assistant to his father, set many of Fanny's hymns to music. Beginning in 1869 with *The Victory*, Hugh ultimately would compile and edit nearly thirty books of hymns and secular songs and write the music to more than a thousand poems. He was a much better musician than Lowry or Doane, and like Fanny he could write sophisticated tunes. But like her, he chose to write hymn melodies more in the popular style, for he believed in "music for the masses."

As we have seen, Van composed the melodies for some of his wife's hymns. Another composer who set several of her poems to music was William F. Sherwin.

One of Fanny's treasured friends was Frances Ridley Havergal, almost seventeen years her junior. The Englishwoman was a widely recognized hymn writer before Fanny began writing for Bradbury. Fanny considered Frances's hymns superior to her own; they included "Who Is on the Lord's Side?" and "Take My Life and Let It Be Consecrated, Lord, to Thee." The two lyricists corresponded regularly, and though they were never able to meet on earth, they were mutual admirers.

ONE OF FANNY'S TREASURED FRIENDS WAS FRANCES RIDLEY HAVERGAL.

The year 1873 marked an end and a beginning. Sylvester Main died at age fifty-six. The beginning was for the work of Dwight L. Moody, who later would figure greatly in Fanny's life. Along with his baritone soloist, Ira D. Sankey, Moody began a series of evangelical meetings in the British Isles, during which thousands professed faith in Christ. Even Alexandra, the Princess of Wales, admitted to being "greatly helped" by Moody's preaching.

Through Sankey's heartrending singing, the British public fell in love with the Sunday school hymn. Sankey used many of Fanny's hymns. "Pass Me Not, O Gentle Saviour" gained sensational popularity. Fanny's name was becoming a household word in Great Britain.

The next year, Fanny was introduced to a tall man with golden hair and beard and a Herculean physique. Philip P. Bliss, the other leading light of American hymnody, had been setting the religious world on fire with his splendid work. Unlike Fanny, he wrote his own tunes and edited his own hymnbooks, which were published by the John Church Company. Only occasionally did he compose tunes for others' poems.

Born in 1838, Bliss had little formal musical training, but he became famous as a music teacher and hymn singer. The title of his hymnal *Gospel Songs* (1874) partly caused the Sunday school hymn to become known as the gospel song or gospel hymn. Bliss wrote the immensely popular march hymn "Hold the Fort" which, along with "Pass Me Not," spread through the British Isles like wildfire.

Bliss's musical talent was far superior to that of any of his contemporaries in the gospel hymn business, with the possible exception of Sankey. His bass voice was rich and powerful. Moody realized he could be of great value in evangelical work, and he urged Bliss to become a full-time evangelist. He wanted to couple Bliss with Daniel Webster Whittle, a layman like Moody and an excellent preacher.

It was a hard decision for Bliss, for he was just getting to the point where he could live comfortably from his royalties. Full-time evangelical work would mean less time for the work he loved best—writing hymns—and less income. But he accepted Moody's direction as God's will and cheerfully undertook his new labors.

The same year, Sankey and Bliss merged some of their hymns to create *Gospel Hymns and Sacred Songs*, published jointly by John Church Company and by Biglow and Main. It was at the beginning of his association with Biglow and Main that Fanny became acquainted with Bliss. She admired his musicianship and perhaps hoped for the opportunity to collaborate with him. However, Bliss then was not looking for any new poems to set to music.

Meanwhile, Fanny was engaged in a speaking tour that took her as far as Cincinnati, where she was a guest at the Doanes' mansion. One evening, she and Doane were talking about the nearness of God. The sun was setting and the evening shadows were gathering. Fanny could see enough to appreciate the beauty and wonder of the scene, which she felt illustrated the glorious hand of God. She was almost ecstatic when she retired, and before she lay down, she wrote the words to "I Am Thine, O Lord." Published the next year in *Brightest and Best*, the hymn immediately became a great favorite.

Indeed, that hymnal produced a bumper crop of hits for Fanny.

> **THAT HYMNAL PRODUCED A BUMPER CROP OF HITS FOR FANNY.**

Also published for the first time were "All the Way My Saviour Leads Me," "Saviour, More Than Life to Me," "To God Be the Glory," and "Yes, There Is Pardon for You." The straightforward "To God Be the Glory," with its simple statement of the Christian faith, was scarcely noticed when published, but it was rediscovered and popularized by Billy Graham in the 1950s.

In 1875, Fanny was fifty-five years old. She and Van now were living on the East Side near the offices of Biglow and Main. An important event was to occur in the religious world of New York that year: Moody and Sankey came to Brooklyn to conduct an evangelical campaign.

12
D. L. MOODY

As early as 7 a.m. on October 24, 1875, the streets were full of people in the vicinity of the Brooklyn Rink. By 9 a.m., when Moody appeared on the platform, the huge building was packed with seven thousand people—most of them young.

The New York Times described Moody as a "well-built man, with a smiling face, a small, shapely head, small features, a full brown beard, and a red face, indicative of jollity and good humor."

"Let us open with the twenty-fourth hymn," he said. At once, he was joined on the platform by a "square-built, solid-looking man with a smiling face, and dark, curly hair, dark moustache, and side whiskers." Ira D. Sankey sat down at the little reed organ and bade the audience, "Please rise and sing heartily!"

After the singing of hymns and a prayer by a local pastor, Moody read from Numbers 13 in his rapid style, with his Yankee twang, describing how the Israelites reached the land of Canaan. Moses' spies reported a land flowing with milk and honey—but inhabited by ferocious giants.

After the reading, Sankey sang "Here I Am! Send Me!" It was the first time New Yorkers had heard the voice that had melted the heart of England. Soon, Sankey had them swaying and sobbing as his glorious baritone resounded through the huge auditorium.

Moody then strode to the lectern to preach on the theme, "Let us go up at once and possess it, for we are well able to overcome it." He talked of a revival in New York City, his sermon punctuated by exclamations of "Yes!" and "Amen!" from the audience. He criticized the unbelief of established churches which, he said, was hindering God's work. He compared those who doubted the possibility of a New York revival to the Israelites afraid to enter the Promised Land. "When we *believe*, we are able to overcome giants and walls and everything!" he exclaimed. The audience went wild.

He closed with this message:

> *If I had the voice of angels, I would like to ask the forty thousand ministers, "Shall we go up to take the land at once?" If we do, we have got to get to work! We have to give way to the Lord. We have to bid farewell to the world—to stop parties and festivals and lectures!*

To this advice, so strange to modern observers—even to many modern believers—came a mighty chorus of amens. Moody asked each of the local ministers who sat on the platform if he were ready. After they all had affirmed, the audience exploded into salvos of "Yes!", "Amen!", and "Hurrah!"

The enthusiasm was fanned to an even more frantic pitch by Sankey's rendition of Bliss's "Only an Armour-Bearer." After the benediction, bands of youths poured from the rink and marched down Fulton Street, arm in arm, singing Bliss's "Hold the Fort, for I Am Coming."

The next afternoon, the entire area of the rink was packed with people, many of whom had crossed the East River from Manhattan. The minute the doors were thrown open, seven thousand men and women fought their way, "crushing, tearing, panting, to the available seats." An equal number were left outside.

Who were these men who had such a profound effect in Scotland and who did so much to spread the hymns of Fanny Crosby over the English-speaking world?

Dwight Lyman Ryther Moody was an uneducated backwoodsman from northern Massachusetts. Born in 1837, he was reared as a Unitarian. In his late teens, while working in a shoe store in Boston, he was converted to orthodox Trinitarian Congregationalism. Later, in Chicago, the aggressive young man easily could have made a fortune in sales, but he decided he best could serve God by selling the Gospel instead.

> WHO WERE THESE MEN WHO DID SO MUCH TO SPREAD THE HYMNS OF FANNY CROSBY OVER THE ENGLISH-SPEAKING WORLD?

During the 1860s, as a YMCA worker, Moody did much to help the poor boys of Chicago's slums. He was so successful that he was asked to hold revival meetings, then evangelistic meetings, or "campaigns," in Britain. Through their success there, Moody and his musician friend Sankey became international celebrities. Moody was never ordained, but by the time of his return from Europe, many Protestant clergymen and laymen looked up to him as their spiritual leader. Until his death, he was perhaps the most important and influential figure in American Protestant churches.

Moody's appeal was not based on personal appearance. At thirty-eight, he stood five feet two inches tall and weighed a solid, muscular 245 pounds, showing no signs of the enormous corpulence that soon would overtake him. He had a small bullet head with coarse, rather unattractive features, which usually were obscured by a gigantic beard. Moody spoke with a heavy New England brogue that many found hard to understand. He spoke rapidly; it was said he pronounced the word *Jerusalem* in one syllable.

He sent both of his sons to Yale, but he did not idolize education. "An educated rascal is the meanest kind of rascal," he maintained. He held biblical commentaries in contempt. "I pore over the pages [of the Bible] not through the specs of some learned commentator, but with my own eyes." Yet Moody, who prayed several hours daily, was loved and respected not only by the ignorant but by many members of the intelligentsia.

Moody was not skilled at all in music. He could play no instrument, and he sang abominably. He loved to hear music, though, and recognized its importance in evangelization. Like Fanny, he believed the Gospel could be sung into the consciousness of people who were not easily moved by preaching. Thus he made it a point to give as much time to the song service as to preaching.

Early in his career, Moody sought a partner to "sing the Gospel" while he preached it. He found such a person in 1870 at a YMCA convention in Indianapolis. The singing was terrible until an obscure revenue official from western Pennsylvania was persuaded to sing. His rendition of "There Is a Fountain Filled with Blood" held the audience spellbound. When the service was over, Moody hunted up the singer, Sankey, and insisted Sankey give up his job and join him in Chicago at once. Sankey, who had a wife and two children, was shocked by the demands of the audacious stranger.

After Sankey returned to Pennsylvania, Moody continued to badger him until he gave in, resigned his job, and moved with his family to Chicago, where he became an inseparable part of Moody's evangelical work. The two men became devoted friends as well as colleagues. Fanny referred to them as David and Jonathan, recalling the close friendship of Israel's future king with the son of King Saul. Until his voice failed, Sankey was given equal billing with Moody, for Moody felt the singer was just as important as the preacher.

Ira David Sankey was born in Edinburg, Pennsylvania, in 1840. Like Moody, he came from a poor family and had almost no formal education. He fought for the Union in the Civil War and often, while in the army, led the singing in the religious services. While working as a revenue agent, he gained local attention as a soloist in the Methodist Church in Newcastle, where he and his wife Fanny were members.

Sankey, five feet ten inches tall and weighing 220 pounds, was suave and polished, in contrast to his rather rough-hewn friend, and loved frock coats and gray silk top hats. He wore the fashionable mutton chop whiskers. Sankey was an emotional man, usually jovial but easily irritated and depressed. He was also somewhat pompous and talkative.

Sankey apparently had a truly beautiful voice and might have been one of the world's finest opera singers. *The New York Times* described his voice as "a rare combination of power and sweetness." But Sankey had no vocal training, and after a few years of campaigning with Moody, his voice was ruined. The first sign of decline was a huskiness that became evident in early 1876. By the time he was forty, his once-magnificent voice was a wreck. The few records he made were done when he was nearly sixty, revealing only a loud, hoarse, booming shell.

These were the men who in the fall of 1875 took New York by storm. Moody and Sankey were less emotional than the run-of-the-mill evangelists of the day. The shouted acclamations at the rink were a far cry from many revivals, where people were known to embrace red-hot stoves, throw themselves on their hands and knees, and imitate the cries of animals.

At this point in his career, Moody emphasized hell much less than many other evangelists. He vigorously opposed Darwin's theory of evolution, but he was less strict about other things. Although he did not smoke, drink, play cards, or even go to the theater, he rarely preached against these things. He was concerned for social justice, and he favored integration. The black faces that dotted the audience and even the platform at the rink startled some New Yorkers. The following year, Moody would become *persona non grata* in the South, accused of trying to change "the relation of the white and black race."

But the revival grew under Moody's preaching and Sankey's singing in the fall and winter of 1875. They campaigned in Philadelphia in November and at the Hippodrome in Manhattan in February. Fanny and Van had moved back to the West Side and had a tenement on Hudson Street. She almost certainly attended many of these meetings. The Hippodrome revivals were received as wildly as those at the Brooklyn Rink had been.

While this was the epoch of the camp meeting and the Bible-thumping evangelist, it also was the day of the medium, séance, and spirit rapper. Evangelical Christians had to contend with a rampant obsession with the occult, as with unbelief. Séances were very popular. In 1863, President Lincoln had held a séance at the White House, consulting the spirits of Washington, Franklin, Lafayette, and other deceased worthies.

Fanny was introduced to Moody and Sankey while they were in New York in 1876, and from then on, her future was indissolubly connected with theirs. Through their appearances, many of her hymns were introduced to a mass audience. And Moody and Sankey were eager for Fanny to supply them with hymns, recognizing her as one of the greatest contemporary hymn writers. Sankey began to fill subsequent editions of *Gospel Hymns and Sacred Songs* with her efforts. Collaborating with Biglow and Main, he obtained the rights

> **FANNY WAS INTRODUCED TO MOODY AND SANKEY WHILE THEY WERE IN NEW YORK IN 1876.**

to many hymns she already had written. He engaged her to write new ones, and he began to write melodies to many of her poems. Though untrained, he often produced melodies of heartrending sweetness.

Fanny spent several days each week at the offices of Biglow and Main, was active in Christian work among the poor and prisoners, and often directed evening activities in tenement houses. She also was receiving many invitations to speak or preach and was traveling a great deal.

Remarkably, she journeyed alone. She would not allow blindness to hinder her activities, and she refused to let people treat her like an invalid.

13
HOME MISSIONS

Any hopes Fanny may have entertained of collaborating with Philip Bliss were dashed forever shortly after Christmas 1876. Bliss and his wife, en route to join an evangelical campaign in Chicago, perished in a train wreck.

The death of Bliss, who was just thirty-eight, "cast a cloud" over Fanny's spirit. Soon she and her colleagues at Biglow and Main were editing his last hymns, a publishing venture jointly undertaken with John Church in Cincinnati. Many of the hymns were incomplete poems that his partner, Major Whittle, sadly undertook to finish. The collection was published in 1877.

Fanny did not confine her literary efforts to sacred songs. She wrote poems to celebrate birthdays, anniversaries, and other events, and she continued to write secular songs. Although she had grown increasingly religious over the past two decades, she still enjoyed writing love lyrics.

At her speaking engagements, which often took her away from New York, her talks were like her hymns: simple, direct, and personal. This quality of intimacy, combined with the love and joy she came to radiate in midlife, made her a popular speaker. On some occasions, lines of people reportedly wrapped around an entire city block, hoping to get in.

Fanny would take the podium with her famous greeting: "God bless your dear hearts! I'm so happy to be with you!" She always held a little book, which many thought contained notes in Braille but which only served, she confided, to give her security. She would say something like this:

> *My friends, I am shut out of the world, and shut in with my Lord! I have served Him as I could. As I have listened to the remarks made tonight [by the person who introduced her], I have thought, "Not unto me, O Lord, but unto Thee, be all the glory!" The Lord is the sunshine of my soul. I do not want to live for myself, but for Him. I remember my grandmother, as I knelt by her chair in which she rocked me to sleep and taught me to pray that if it was His will, to give me what I wanted, but if the Lord did not want me to have the things, it is best not to.*
>
> *My friends, it is so good to be loved! Loved by God's own people! The memory of this meeting will never fade from my mind! When I go home and look into my Father's face and see the sunshine of His smile, my feelings will be like the tender affection and gratitude that glows in my heart now for you.*

Short, rambling, but sincere and inspiring—such was the character of her addresses. She almost always recited one or more of her poems and sometimes would compose one spontaneously for the occasion. She always closed with the Mizpah benediction: "May the Lord watch between me and thee, when we are absent, one from the other."

She radiated an aura of warmth, of holiness—something that

transcended the brevity and simplicity of her remarks and was enough to incite people from all walks of life to stand all day in stifling heat or bitter cold to hear her. She could cheer the despondent, arouse the lukewarm to a greater sense of commitment, and inspire the agnostic to make the decision for Christ. Although she spoke to smaller audiences than some of her friends because she insisted on minimal publicity, in many ways she was becoming one of the most effective evangelists of her day.

SHE RADIATED AN AURA OF WARMTH, OF HOLINESS.

Though small and somewhat delicate, Fanny had boundless energy and was never seriously ill. Even in extreme old age, she would tire out people twenty to thirty years younger. But even she needed a vacation at least once a year, so in the summer of 1877, she attended the Methodist Episcopal Church camp meeting at Ocean Grove, New Jersey. It was founded by pastors from New York, Philadelphia, and Trenton who sought a summer resort "free from the fashion and folly" of most amusement parks. Along with recreation, they wanted to be able to hold religious exercises. The faithful could come to swim, fish, and wander along the beach but also to hear the Word of God proclaimed in three or more services each day. Preachers of all denominations spoke at Ocean Grove. The vacationers rented tents that were often so small one was obliged to enter on hands and knees.

Fanny had never had the money to rent an Ocean Grove tent, but in 1877, she attended as an "honored guest" of friends, probably the Knapps. She made the two-hour trip by train, alone. As usual, she made friends on the train, and a kind passenger escorted her to her friends' tent.

The highlight of the camp meeting was the evening Surf Meeting. At sunset, the faithful trooped down to the beach to be led in a moving vesper service. Although she could see but a few faint hues of the sunset, Fanny was just as moved as her sighted friends.

Here she made some important contacts. The song leader was John Robson Sweney. A stout, balding man with heavy-lidded eyes, mustache, and goatee, Sweney was well known as both band leader and hymn writer. Born in 1837, Sweney had studied vocal music and had been in charge of a regimental band during the Civil War. Afterward, he organized Sweney's Cornet Band in Philadelphia and taught music at the Pennsylvania Music Academy.

A Presbyterian, Sweney led the singing at a number of evangelical camp meetings around the country. Specializing in light, bouncy, rollicking tunes, he had composed popular hymns and published several hymnals, which included poems by Fanny. Now he met her for the first time and asked her to supply the words for more of his tunes.

So did William James Kirkpatrick, Sweney's friend and colleague. A happy, vivacious, warm man born in Pennsylvania in 1838, Kirkpatrick had been trained in vocal music, the pipe organ, harmony, theory, and composition. The "Professor," as he was called, was much better trained as a musician than many of his hymn-writing contemporaries. In Philadelphia, he had become a successful furniture dealer, composing music on the side. He recently had joined Sweney in publishing hymn books for a Philadelphia firm.

Fanny, with her strong sense of humor, much enjoyed the company of "Kirkie." She would supply Sweney and Kirkpatrick with nearly a thousand hymns for the books they edited. Also during this period, Fanny began to supply Sankey with poems for his *Gospel Hymns*, which in the next decade would run to six volumes.

About this time in New York, Fanny met still another composer:

a six-foot, gaunt man with pince-nez spectacles and a neat goatee. Quiet, gentle, and restrained, George Coles Stebbins was unlike the gregarious Kirkpatrick. Born on a farm in Orleans County, New York, in 1846, Stebbins as a musician was largely self-taught, but he acquired a considerable reputation as a choirmaster when, in 1876, Moody called him to evangelistic work. Stebbins readily responded and was paired with a preacher named George Pentecost.

Over the next few decades, Stebbins would set many of Fanny's poems to music. He did not always do a good job; his style was sometimes monotonous, awkward, and unmelodic. However, he did write some very appealing hymn tunes. With Fanny, he wrote "Jesus Is Calling" and "Saved by Grace."

By this time, Fanny had created most of her most famous hymns. In nine years, she had written "Safe in the Arms of Jesus," "Blessed Assurance," "Pass Me Not, O Gentle Saviour," "Jesus, Keep Me Near the Cross," "I Am Thine, O Lord," "All the Way My Saviour Leads Me," "Close to Thee," "Praise Him! Praise Him!," "To God Be the Glory," "Every Day and Hour," and "Rescue the Perishing." In later years, with two or three possible exceptions, none of her hymns would equal these in popularity.

Why was this? Had she burned out?

Most likely, yes. Fanny Crosby had said everything she had to say. Almost everything she would produce henceforth would paraphrase something written earlier.

But she was by no means washed up as a hymn writer. Even her paraphrases gained moderate popularity and often were superior to the lyrics of many contemporaries. She was in ever-increasing demand as a lyricist.

The fact that her current hymns were not as popular as earlier ones did not trouble Fanny. She knew she was doing the Lord's work and felt certain her hymns would be helpful to some people. If they led just one person to Christ, she would be content.

What did bother her was that some of what she considered to be her best poems were not set to music. She often complained that her musi-

> **THE FACT THAT HER CURRENT HYMNS WERE NOT AS POPULAR AS EARLIER ONES DID NOT TROUBLE FANNY.**

cian friends ignored her best and set to music her worst lyrics. Unfortunately, few of these unused lyrics have survived. Those which have were clearly too complicated to be treated adequately by the musicians who usually worked with her. The lyrics would not have made "music for the masses."

In the spring of 1879, Frances Havergal, Fanny's friend by correspondence, fell ill and died in Wales at forty-two. Fanny was nearly sixty and had outlived both friends—Philip Bliss and Frances—who, with her, had spearheaded the lyrical wing of the gospel hymn movement. Their premature deaths left Fanny unrivaled as the "queen of gospel hymn writers," as she now was known. Until her death, Fanny would be the patron saint of hymnody for evangelical Protestants.

She made regular trips to Bridgeport, where her mother and sisters lived. Mercy Morris, alert and vigorous at eighty, lived with her daughter Carolyn. Fanny's other sister, Julia, lived nearby, working as a dressmaker to support her disabled husband, Byron.

Fanny at sixty was more active than most men or women at forty. She recently had begun what became a second career, parallel to her hymn writing, as a home mission worker. She now spent several days a week in the missions of New York's Bowery district.

14
THE BOWERY

The plight of the thousands living in New York's tenements long had been a concern for many Christians. For years, dedicated individuals had toiled to help the miserable inhabitants in the morass of Manhattan's slums, but with little obvious effect.

In the early 1880s, Fanny was living in a dismal flat on Frankfort Street on the Lower East Side, near one of Manhattan's worst slums. Just a few blocks away stretched the notorious Bowery, one of America's most depressing places, a haunt for hopeless alcoholics and the main artery of a thriving commercial area, red light district, and pornographic center. Here were taverns, dance halls, and sordid shops selling filthy pictures and literature. "Concert halls" specialized in cheap, degrading, burlesque shows. "Dime museums" lured the curious to view gross indecencies. In one place, admission was charged to see a man named Jack the Rat bite the heads off living rats. Organ grinders, harpers, and dancing bears swarmed the streets. Bedraggled prostitutes, "so worn, raddled, and hideous that their appeal to men was inconceivable," strutted to and fro. Along the way were human wrecks of the Civil

> **FANNY WAS LIVING IN A DISMAL FLAT NEAR ONE OF MANHATTAN'S WORST SLUMS.**

War—men without arms, legs, eyes, or noses whose only livelihood was begging.

The neighborhood was so terrible that people from better areas of the city would hire carriages and, taking a detective for a guide, ride through the area for sordid sightseeing.

Christian workers long had toiled in this district, with few results. The John Street Methodist Church nearby encouraged its laymen to work among the wretched, but they often met with frustration.

In the typical home mission of the 1870s, a full-time team of Christian workers ministered to the down and out. One of the first and most important was the Water Street Mission, located near the East River almost under the shadow of the still-incomplete Brooklyn Bridge. It was founded by a remarkable Irishman, Jeremiah McAuley. Coming from a broken home, he was never educated and remained practically illiterate until he died. At fourteen, he was sent to live with relatives in New York City, where he soon became a member of a street gang. At nineteen, he was convicted mistakenly of highway robbery and served five years at Sing Sing Penitentiary before he could establish his innocence and obtain freedom. During his term, he was converted from nominal Roman Catholicism to fervent Methodism through the efforts of Orville "Awful" Gardner, a prize fighter converted at the beginning of the revivals, who had devoted his life to working with prisoners.

After his discharge, with no friends to give him moral support, Jerry McAuley once again slipped back into the life of a drifter and bum. After several attempts, he finally reformed while in his late twenties.

McAuley became a devoted member of the John Street Methodist Church. He was very concerned about men caught in a plight like his own, and he founded the mission in 1872. Ten years later he opened the Cremorne-McAuley Mission on West Thirty-second Street. In this three-story building with a chapel, kitchen, and living quarters, the homeless and unemployed were fed and clothed. The men shared meals with Jerry and his wife, Maria, upstairs.

Apart from the religious services, where McAuley or an outside speaker would urge the men to enter into a personal relationship with Christ, the guests were not prodded or coerced into religion. Some mission workers tried to make the men promise to become Christians before giving them food or clothes, but not the McAuleys.

Prison authorities came to respect McAuley's work. When a man had served his term at Sing Sing, he usually was advised, "You had better go down and see McAuley at the Water Street Mission."

Fanny heard about McAuley and frequently visited the mission. She was much impressed by its founder. "As a speaker, he used simple language, but his manner was so impressive that all men were drawn to him."

She also became acquainted with other rescue missions. In 1879, Rev. Albert Rulifson founded the Bowery Mission on Bowery Street, and in the early 1880s, the hymn writer became a regular visitor there. She also appeared frequently at Mrs. E. M. Whittemore's Door of Hope, an establishment for "fallen women."

Fanny was not a passive spectator. Sometimes she would be asked to give the address. She would tell of the joy it gave to walk in the light and urge the men to come forward and give their lives to Christ. More often, she would go sit in the audience,

FANNY WOULD SIT IN THE AUDIENCE, MINGLING WITH THE MEN AND WOMEN.

mingling with the men and women. Her conversational counseling was immensely successful.

On one occasion at the Bowery Mission, she delivered the address, closing with, "If there is a man present who has gone as far as he can go, he is the person with whom I want to shake hands."

Sure enough, a man appeared. When the meeting was over, Fanny asked him if he wanted "to come out and live a Christian life."

"Aw, what's the difference?" he asked. "I ain't got no friends. Nobody cares for me."

"You're mistaken," Fanny replied, "for the Lord Jesus cares for you—and others care, too! Unless I had a deep interest in your soul's welfare, I certainly would not be here talking with you on this subject."

She gave him several scripture passages. The man seemed to be interested and said he would come the next evening and sign the pledge not to use alcohol. Would she come with him?

"Yes," she said. "I will be here again tomorrow. But although I don't want to discourage you for signing the pledge, it seems to me that the best pledge you can give is to yield yourself to God."

The man appeared the next evening and, "before the close of the meeting, we saw the new light in his eyes and felt the change in his voice."

After she was sixty, Fanny considered her chief occupation that of a home mission worker. Hymn writing was but an extension of her mission work. Many of her hymns were written expressly for use in the missions, urging one to make a decision, describing the joys of a relationship with Jesus, or offering hope to the downcast.

Love was the hallmark of her work. She never served in any official or employed capacity but gave her time freely.

"Don't tell me a man is a sinner," she always insisted. "You can't save a man by telling him of his sins. He knows them already. Tell him there is pardon and love waiting for him. Win his confidence and make him understand that you believe in him, and never give him up!"

Those were her guidelines for mission.

Kindness, she said, helps others not only to come to faith, "but to grow in grace, day by day. There are many timid souls whom we jostle morning and evening, as we pass them by. But if only a kind word were spoken, they might become fully persuaded."

Fanny was diligent not to hurt anyone's feelings in her mission work. All the men with whom she worked were "my boys."

FANNY WAS DILIGENT NOT TO HURT ANYONE'S FEELINGS IN HER MISSION WORK.

Of the trainmen with whom she worked closely through the YMCA for many years, she said, "They are *all* my boys, and I love them all!" Of the men at the Bowery and Water Street missions, most of whom reeked of alcohol and tobacco and swarmed with vermin after weeks without a bath, she said, "Not one of them was ever ugly to me."

The Bowery Mission, sponsored by *The Christian Herald* periodical, was her pet mission, and she spent more time there than in any other. She spoke at sixteen annual anniversary services, when those converted and rehabilitated by its ministry appeared as guests of honor.

In 1880, Fanny was invited to the home of her friend William Rock, president of the New York Surface Car Line. A pious man, Rock was concerned about his employees. These men had a hard lot, working seven days a week. They received few kind words and little fellowship but much abuse from testy riders. Because of the work and the wages, Surface Line employees tended to be a gruff, surly lot. Rock, however, felt some provision should be made for their spiritual welfare, and he consulted Fanny.

A waiting room was prepared for an hour-long service each Sunday morning for conductors and drivers. Rock asked Fanny to conduct the services. In a "dingy little room made cheerful with a bit of red carpet and a few flowers and plants," she began the mission with her "railroad boys." As elsewhere, her sermons were of love and consolation.

Her work with the streetcar conductors and bus drivers made a great impression in New York. The following year, a delegation called on her from the newly formed Railroad Branch of the YMCA, centered across the Hudson in Hoboken, New Jersey. They asked her to become a regular lecturer for their organization. For the rest of her active life, she undertook speaking tours at YMCAs along the East Coast.

Fanny also was active in temperance work. She felt half the battle for the soul of the down-and-out was won if a way could be found to stop the drinking. She had seen what a curse beer, wine, and whiskey were in the Lower Manhattan tenements. She had observed alcohol's effects while working with the railroad men and streetcar conductors. She knew how it led to disastrous marital problems and broken homes.

Fanny was totally against the use of alcohol. Perhaps certain people could use it in moderation, but she felt so many others could not that it was far better to encourage total abstinence.

Her solution was the temperance pledge. If one never used liquor, there was no danger of becoming a slave to it. She never identified abstinence with Christian faith or equated signing the pledge with a religious commitment. She believed, however, that total abstinence from alcoholic beverages was a goal any intelligent Christian should aim for.

Moody felt the same way, as did most religious leaders of the day. Total abstinence long had been popular in the Roman Catholic Church. Among those who worked in the missions, those who had seen the full effects of alcoholism, this feeling was especially strong. Jerry McAuley and his associate Sam Hadley were both recovered alcoholics and were "dead against" all liquid intoxicants.

Biglow and Main published many temperance hymns in those years, including an entire temperance hymnal, *The Tidal Wave*, with songs by Fanny, Annie Hawks, Josephine Pollard, Robert Lowry, and others.

Temperance and all her other activities were linked inextricably to the hymn writing by which Fanny sang her faith and her ideas into the hearts of thousands.

Fanny wrote most of her hymns after midnight; only then did she have the absolute silence required for perfect concentration. The constant shuffle of feet on rickety wooden floors, the strident

FANNY WROTE MOST OF HER HYMNS AFTER MIDNIGHT.

babble of several languages piercing the thin walls, and the shouts and curses of drunken, quarreling tenants precluded any mental work. Since Fanny was never much of a sleeper, the lateness of the hour did not bother her. Her entire days and evenings were occupied at Biglow and Main, in social work or, increasingly, in public appearances.

Her hymn writing was connected inextricably with her mysticism. When the tenement noises had died away and she sat alone, Fanny entered into prayer and arrived at a meditative state she often referred to as "the Valley of Silence." She believed she entered into direct communion with the spiritual world, often feeling her soul sally forth from her body in ethereal reverie. In the rapture and ecstasy of "Deep Meditation," as she called it, Fanny often felt she could hear the unearthly harmonies of "the Celestial Choirs." She claimed she felt the presence not only of Christ and His saints and angels but of relatives and friends who had "passed beyond the silent vale."

So meditating, she often received inspiration for her hymns. Toward the end of her life, she wrote in a poem:

In the hush of the Valley of Silence,
I dream all the songs that I sing,
And the music floats down the dim valley
'Til each finds a word for a wing,
That, to men, like the dove of the Deluge,
The message of peace they may bring.

Sometimes her soul was flooded with inspiration so powerful she could not "find words beautiful enough, or thoughts deep enough, for expression."

While it was in the Valley of Silence that many of her hymns were inspired, others received initial inspiration from events in the material world. She frequently was given a hymn topic by one of her musician friends. She would keep a subject in mind as she went about her affairs, sometimes for days, weeks, or months, until something happened to interest her in writing about it. The death of a friend might lead to a hymn such as "The Morning Land." Something that occurred at a mission might draw her to the subject of "The Blessed Feast."

One day in 1874, Fanny was at a loss as to how she would pay her rent, so she decided to pray for it. Just then a man appeared whom she had never met. He left at once after pressing a ten-dollar bill into her hand—the exact amount of the rent. This inspired a hymn based on a topic Lowry had given her: "All the Way My Saviour Leads Me." That night, the words flowed:

> *All the way my Saviour leads me;*
> *What have I to ask beside?*
> *Can I doubt His tender mercy*
> *Who through life has been my guide?*

She did not necessarily need a theme in advance. A chance remark or event could be her inspiration. A twilight talk while staying with the Doanes in Cincinnati led her to write "I Am Thine, O Lord."

Sankey once told her about a miner who had come forward in one of the campaigns in England and begged to be prayed for. The leader of the postservice prayer meeting, perhaps because it was getting late, suggested the miner come again the next night. But the miner cried piteously, "No! It must be settled tonight! Tomorrow may be too late!" The leader gave in, and the miner left the meeting "saved." The next day he perished in an explosion.

Fanny was so moved that she composed a hymn called "Shall I Be Saved To-Night?"

On another occasion, Fanny was a guest of William and Sara Kirkpatrick in Germantown, Pennsylvania. Along with other guests, they were discussing the transitory nature of earthly life.

"How soon we grow weary of earthly pleasures, however bright they may be," Fanny mused.

"Well," said the professor, "we are. . .never weary of the grand old song!"

"WE ARE NEVER WEARY OF THE GRAND OLD SONG!"

Fanny instantly seized upon the rhythm of the words as ideal for a hymn. She startled everybody by suddenly crying, "But what comes next?"

Her host paused, somewhat confused.

"Why, glory to God, hallelujah!" Fanny continued. She insisted that Kirkie seat himself at the piano to compose an appropriate tune to the words she dictated on the spot:

> *We are never, never weary of the grand old song,*
> *Glory to God, hallelujah!*
> *We can sing it in the Spirit as we march along,*
> *Glory to God, hallelujah!*

Later in life, shortly after her mother died, the poet had a vision in which Mercy spoke to her from "beyond the river." That night, Fanny was moved to compose this verse:

> *Over the river they call me,*
> *Friends that are dear to my heart,*
> *Soon I shall meet them in glory,*
> *Never, no never to part.*

In 1874, in a spell of deep depression, she cried out, "Dear Lord, hold my hand!" She wrote, "Almost at once, the sweet peace that comes of perfect assurance returned to my heart, and my gratitude for the evidence of answered prayer sang itself into the lines of the hymn":

Hold Thou my hand, so weak am I and helpless
I dare not take one step without Thy aid;
Hold Thou my hand, for then, oh, loving Saviour,
No dread of ill shall make my soul afraid.

Sometimes, as in the case of "Blessed Assurance," "Safe in the Arms of Jesus," and others, a composer would play a tune and ask her to write words for it. Fanny would listen, and if the tune "said something," she could write a hymn. But it was very important what the tune "said." After she listened to it once or twice, she might tell the composer, "No, I cannot write any words for this. The tune does not *say* anything."

Biglow and Main required her to write on many topics that did not inspire her at all. She was expected to supply a quota of hymns regardless of whether she felt like writing. She confessed that "there are some days, or at least hours, when I could not compose a hymn if all the world were laid at my feet as a promised recompense."

"Give me a New Year's hymn," Doane might demand on December 30. "Fan, I'd like you to compose twenty selections for my Easter collection," Hugh Main might say, "and I'd like them in two weeks." "I'd like three invitational hymns for my services," Jerry McAuley might request.

MOST OF THE HYMNS SHE WROTE WERE UNINSPIRED; SHE HAD TO FORCE HERSELF TO WRITE THEM.

Since Fanny seldom refused, she would have to "build a mood—or try to draw one around me."

Hymn writing was difficult if she had no inspiration. She would "pray to God to give me the thoughts and feelings wherewith to write my hymn." Then, "after a time—perhaps not unmingled with struggle—the ideas. . .come." Indeed, most of the hymns she wrote were uninspired; she had to force herself to write them.

While writing hymns, Fanny had a peculiar habit of holding a little book upside down in front of her face. This was a ritual, apparently like that of a baseball pitcher who will not shave the day he pitches or the prima donna who will not go onstage unless she kisses her mother's picture. For Fanny, it was a superstitious habit, like her practice of always carrying a miniature silk American flag. She claimed, "Words seem to come more promptly when the little volume is in my grasp."

The contents of the book seemed less important to her than the size and shape. Often she used a Bible, prayer book, or psaltery—or even a secular book. She liked a book small enough that her long, slender fingers could fit around it.

When trying to compose a hymn for which she was not inspired, she prayed, and when she was "sure that I am in condition to reach the minds and hearts of my constituency and sing them something worthy for them to hear," she began working with the measure and melody. She often used a popular tune like "Sweet Hour of Prayer" or "Stand Up, Stand Up for Jesus" as the model on which to construct her verses.

The hymn had to be constructed for maximum singability. How she constructed the meter and placed the accents was very important. "For if there is a false accent or a mistake in metre, the hymn cannot stand much chance of proving a success; or, at least, its possibilities are very much lessened. Among the millions of hymns that have been sung and forgotten, many, no doubt, contain deep and pious thought and feeling, but have been crippled or killed by the roughness of some line, or the irregularity of one or more measures."

If no tune was provided already, or if she did not think of one already existing on which to hang the words, she carefully tried to construct her verses "in such a manner that the composer of the music may readily grasp the spirit of the poem and compose notes that will perfect the expression of the poet's meaning." This was a problem, for, as we have seen, many of the men who set her words to music were amateurs. There was no problem of this sort when a tune was provided, as Fanny was a master versifier and had no trouble composing verses for specific tunes.

She preferred to have a tune rather than a topic. If the tune were good, she could write a good poem; if it were bad, she could reject it. If she wrote a good poem to a given topic, she could not be sure it would be given a good tune.

When a poem came from divine inspiration, it came to Fanny as a whole and quite rapidly. Otherwise, it came slower. Her hymns often came by stanzas and, in many instances, verse by verse. When she was not inspired, she often had to labor for hours to get a satisfactory poem. With "The Bright Forever," she struggled two days without coming up with a single line. Suddenly, "almost in a twinkling, the words came, stanza by stanza, as fast as I could memorize them."

WHEN A POEM CAME FROM DIVINE INSPIRATION, IT CAME TO FANNY AS A WHOLE AND QUITE RAPIDLY.

Usually, she completed the first draft in a single night, often after two or three hours. If there were time, she "let it lie for a few days in the writing-desk of my mind, so to speak, until I have the leisure to prune it, to read through it with the eyes of my memory, and, in other ways, mould it into as presentable shape as possible."

But she did not always have time to prune and revise because of pressure from publishers to provide multiple poems in a short time. Her habit of composing two or three poems for every topic or tune heightened the pressure. Thus the large majority of Fanny's nine thousand hymns were written in great haste and, as hymnologist John Julian characterized, were "weak and poor." But on those rare occasions when Fanny was inspired and could take her time, the hymns were often of excellent quality.

During these years of mass writing, Fanny dictated lines to a secretary. Hugh Main described Fanny's very unusual work methods: "She has her hymns written down for her and will dictate to two persons at once, or two lines of *one* poem to one person, and two lines of *another* hymn to *another* person and never forgets herself."

People marveled at her wonderful memory. They were dumbfounded at her ability to commit a seemingly endless number of hymns to memory and dictate them without apparent difficulty, one after another. But whenever they made a great deal of this "talent," Fanny would give them a lecture, maintaining she simply was using a gift—memory—which God gives to everyone, but which most people with sight lose through laziness. She criticized "memorandum tablets and carefully kept journals and ledgers" as destructive to "the books of the mind."

For each hymn, Fanny was paid a dollar or two by Biglow and Main and most other publishing houses. No matter how successful the hymn might turn out to be, she would get nothing more. The words became the exclusive property of the composer, and no one else could set them to music.

In most instances, even the composer made comparatively

little money from the hymn. The publishing company received most of the profits. Through the years, many people felt Fanny was being exploited, and she was urged to insist on a higher wage for her services. But she felt that in writing hymns, she was doing a favor for her friends. More importantly, she was doing God's work. Her recompense was the number of souls being led to God through the hymns.

15
"THE TOP 10"

Had there been a rating for popular songs in the last two decades of the nineteenth century, several of Fanny's hymns certainly would have been in the Top 10. For nearly a decade, "Safe in the Arms of Jesus" had been a universal favorite; within another twenty years it would be translated into more than two hundred languages and sung the world over. "Blessed Assurance" also had attained immense popularity. Ira Sankey said it was "one of the most popular and useful" of all the hymns he and Moody used in their campaigns.

The number-one hit of their meetings was "Pass Me Not, O Gentle Saviour," of which Sankey wrote: "No other hymn in our collection was more popular than this at our meetings in London in 1874. It was sung every day at Her Majesty's Theatre in Pall Mall." It, too, was translated into several languages. After the return of the evangelists to the states, "Pass Me Not" continued to be the most popular hymn of the campaigns. Dr. E. I. Dakin, a prominent New York Baptist clergyman, credited it with bringing more people to Christ than any other hymn.

> THE NUMBER 1 HIT WAS "PASS ME NOT, O GENTLE SAVIOUR."

"Rescue the Perishing," "Jesus, Keep Me Near the Cross," "I Am Thine, O Lord," and "All the Way My Saviour Leads Me" likewise were tremendous hits.

The hymns were popular in secular circles as well as religious, alongside such favorites as "Silver Threads Among the Gold," "When You and I Were Young, Maggie," and "In the Good Old Summer-Time." Through the universal appeal of her hymns, by her sixth decade Fanny was beginning to realize her ambition of winning a million men to Christ. Reports abounded of how people were moved to the point of conversion by her simple but earnest lyrics.

Fanny was eager to hear of news of conversions inspired by her hymns, not for the sake of pride but because she felt it was evidence of the workings of God. "God has given me a wonderful work to do," she said, "a work that has brought me untold blessing and great joy. When word is brought to me, as it is from time to time, of some wandering soul being brought home through one of my hymns, my heart thrills with joy, and I give thanks to God for giving me a share in the glorious work of saving human souls."

Fanny's hymns not only helped convert the indifferent and unbelieving; they also were of great comfort to those who already believed. "You have been the means of cheering tens of thousands trudging along the highways of life," Sankey once told her.

One day a woman came up to Fanny after church and cried, "Oh, thank God I have found you. I have prayed that I might see you before I die. 'Safe in the Arms of Jesus' was the last thing my mother said before she went home." Sankey brought a similar account back from Scotland in 1885. "Safe in the Arms of Jesus" had led to conversions and consoled many in crisis.

"Blessed Assurance" also had great effect. A teenage boy,

hospitalized with an incurable illness, was said to have converted fourteen other patients by his singing of "Blessed Assurance." Later, as his own dying moment approached, he fervently sang "Safe in the Arms of Jesus." Just as his soul departed, he cried out, "Ma, I hear the voice of angels! Ma, there are the fields of glory! Ma, there is the jasper sea!"

"Rescue the Perishing" led to many conversions, although it was directed toward Christians, stirring them to win unconverted souls. An alcoholic aimlessly wandering through the Bowery passed the Water Street Mission one day and heard worshippers singing the hymn. Attracted to the lilting, forceful hymn, he went inside to hear it better. When it was over, he "broke down in contrition."

> "RESCUE THE PERISHING" LED TO MANY CONVERSIONS, ALTHOUGH IT WAS DIRECTED TOWARD CHRISTIANS.

An Englishman wrote to Sankey attributing "my conversion, through the grace of God, to one verse of that precious hymn, 'Rescue the Perishing.' " He said he was "very far from my Saviour and living without a hope in Jesus. Yet I was very fond of singing hymns, and one day I came across this beautiful piece." He cited especially this passage:

Touched by a loving heart,
Wakened by kindness,
Chords that were broken will vibrate once more.

One evening at the Bowery Mission, a ragged, drunk man staggered in. "Rescue the Perishing" was being sung and made a great impression on the poor wretch. During the sermon, the speaker referred to his Civil War experiences and mentioned the name of the company with which he served.

After the service, the drunkard reeled up to the speaker and sputtered, "Do you remember the name of the captain of your company at that time?" The speaker quoted the name. "You are right," said the bum, emotionally. "I am that man! *I* was your captain! Now, look at me today and see what a wreck I am! I have lost everything in the world that I had through drink, and I don't know where to go. Can you save your old captain?"

The drunk veteran was converted that evening and afterward became a devoted mission worker. He gave many lectures telling of his conversion and attributing his change of heart to the hymn "Rescue the Perishing."

"Pass Me Not" likewise was said to have led to many conversions. Sankey wrote of the prominent Englishman who "had been very much opposed to our meetings, and his opposition was not lessened when he saw his wife converted." But the man agreed to accompany his wife to the last meeting. He was so moved by the words of "Pass Me Not" that he felt "touched by the Spirit of God."

Many were moved by some of Fanny's lesser-known works. In the early 1870s, she was on a trolley with Howard Doane when the inspiration suddenly came. Right then, she wrote a hymn beginning:

Jesus, I love Thee, Thou art to me
Dearer than ever mortal can be;
Jesus, I love Thee, Saviour Divine,
Earth has no friendship constant as Thine;

Thou wilt forgive me when I am wrong,
Thou art my comfort, Thou art my song!
Jesus, I love Thee, yes, Thou art mine.
Living or dying, still I am Thine!

Doane was moved and set the words to music that evening. It was published in 1873 and became moderately popular. Moody and Sankey used it during their British campaigns. A British Methodist pastor used it as an invitational hymn during an evening service several years later. After the singing, a visitor surrendered herself to the Lord. She became one of the most devoted members that congregation had ever known. She felt the words to Fanny's hymn had enlightened her soul, and she wanted others to know and share the joy she felt in Jesus Christ. She was such an energetic, effective witness that before her death a year later, she had led twenty-four persons to make a personal commitment to Christ and join the church. On her deathbed, she asked her pastor to thank Fanny Crosby for writing the hymn.

Another moderately popular hymn was responsible for a conversion in the South. A country squire, though indifferent to matters of faith, loved to listen to hymns. One night he was in town and decided to stop by the local church, where a prayer meeting was in progress. He heard just one hymn, "Only a Step to Jesus." It moved him so greatly he could not put it from his mind. He dreamed about the words that night, and the next day he began to think about their meaning and examine his life. Soon, he was a committed believer. He went to the church and related his experience. Many of the faithful, who had never expected this man to display the slightest interest in religion, wept openly.

Around 1900, a Pittsburgh Anglican church was jolted when

a woman went forward to "testify"—an unheard-of thing in an Anglican Mass. Before the astonished priests and parishioners, she told of her life as a woman of easy virtue who happened to hear "Saved by Grace" at an open-air meeting. It reminded her of her childhood and her mother's constant prayers for her. The woman fell to her knees on the curbstone and asked God's pardon. "Then and there I received it, and I left the place with a peace which has never forsaken me."

The rector descended from the high altar and, with tears in his eyes, bid her Godspeed. Parishioners said the feeling was so intense "the Lord Jesus and His Mother have been here."

What was there about these simple hymns, set to even more simple tunes, that deeply affected so many? Fanny attributed it to the Holy Spirit. Whenever she wrote a hymn, she prayed God would use it to lead many souls to Him. She prayed she might be the means of saving a million men through her hymns.

> **WHAT WAS THERE ABOUT THESE SIMPLE HYMNS THAT DEEPLY AFFECTED SO MANY?**

Although the hymns were not first-rate literature, they could produce great emotional effect. They were straightforward, usually simple enough for a child to understand, yet not as trite as most hymns of the time. She made them vivid through the use of familiar phrases. Terms like "sylvan bowers" and "vernal flowers" make for the worst of poetry—but for very successful hymnody. Fanny considered hymnody not "pure" poetry but more utilitarian, intended to facilitate worship.

So she filled hymns with familiar phrases: "Rock of Ages," "saved by grace," "golden shore," "bleeding side." Most of her hymns alluded to scripture: "living bread" (John 6:35), waters "gushing from the rock" (Numbers 20:11), "my Father's house above" (John 14:2), "the angel reapers" gathering in the harvest (Matthew 13:39), the "pearly gates" (Revelation 21:21), and so on. A curious exception to this practice was her use of "summerland," taken from spiritualism and referring to the dwelling place of the happy dead.

Fanny defined a hymn as "a song of the heart addressed to God," and her hymns were dear to the hearts of those who sang them. She related her hymns to the worshipper's own experience: "Now there is pardon for *you*." "Pass *me* not." "*I* come to Thee, *I* come to Thee." Fanny wrote most of her hymns in the first person so those who sang them might become more intimately involved in their thoughts.

One of the most striking things about her hymns is the familiarity with which the Saviour is addressed. She uses the "familiar and fondling epithets" so decried by Lowell Mason; even in modern times, some find this aspect of her hymnody objectionable. One reason she took this approach was her belief in a strong, intensely personal relationship with God. It also must be remembered that she lived in

> ONE OF THE MOST STRIKING THINGS ABOUT HER HYMNS IS THE FAMILIARITY WITH WHICH THE SAVIOUR IS ADDRESSED.

an emotional age, when affection was more openly acknowledged than today. Tears rolled down Sankey's cheeks when he sang. Men wept profusely in public.

Partly because she was blind, no doubt, physical contact meant a lot to Fanny. She was always hugging and kissing and greeting everyone with, "God bless your dear heart! I'm so happy to see you!" The Bowery bums and railroad men were "my boys," Carrie and Jule "my precious, darling sisters," Kirkpatrick "Kirkie," her friend Adelbert White the "dear deacon."

Since Fanny addressed relatives and companions in emotionally affectionate language, it was very natural for her to address her Savior the same way. After all, she loved Him more than anyone else.

In addition to emotion, Fanny used the device of repetition. She tended to repeat a key phrase, word, or figure of speech throughout a hymn—the same technique modern advertising writers use for subliminal impression. In "Safe in the Arms of Jesus," for example, the word "safe" is repeated five times in three stanzas and is found twice in the chorus. Worshippers are unaware the word is being implanted inexorably in their minds, but afterward, their subconscious tells them they are "safe" in Jesus' arms.

Some people have claimed the success of Fanny's hymns resulted more from the tunes than the words. The various accounts of conversions through her hymns would tend to disprove that. In most instances, it was the words that stuck with the hearer; the tune was the vehicle. Lowry often said the words usually carried more effect than the music.

Criticism did not trouble Fanny. She was writing not for the critics but for the common people. She knew what type of hymn the common person could best understand.

16
WRITTEN OUT

With the opening of the Brooklyn Bridge in May 1883, it became fairly easy for those who worked in busy New York City to commute to the more suburban city of Brooklyn. Many people bought or built homes across the East River, among them George Coles Stebbins and his wife and son, who moved from Chicago. Around the same time, Ira Sankey brought his wife and sons from Chicago. Fanny now had an opportunity to know both families more intimately. The gentle, quiet Stebbins became one of her "most devoted and precious friends."

Fanny was frequently a guest at the Stebbinses' home, but more often the two met at the Sankeys' home. The high-strung Sankey was similar in temperament to Fanny. For the next decade and a half, she was a regular guest in the Sankeys' spacious parlor. Next to Moody, she may have been Sankey's closest friend.

She and Sankey began to write more hymns together, many of them at the Sankeys' reed organ. Sankey set her poems to his simple but plaintively melodious airs. He and Phoebe Knapp probably were her closest friends at this time.

In 1883 or 1884, Fanny moved uptown to First Avenue and Seventy-ninth Street. Now too far away to attend the John Street Methodist Church, she began to frequent and eventually joined the

Cornell Memorial Church on Seventy-sixth Street. It was the first church she ever officially had joined. Perhaps she felt she was at an age when it was wise to be affiliated with a congregation, if for no other reason than to be assured of having a clergyman to conduct her burial service!

Whether she was still with Van at this time is in question. It is certain he no longer figured prominently in her life. As of 1882, the couple was still together, but because of different interests and circles of friends, perhaps compounded by a waning of physical passion with the advancing years, the two blind musicians were growing apart. There apparently was no overt unhappiness between them, but they were less often in each other's company. They still loved each other, according to Fanny, but gradually the relationship was downgraded, by mutual consent, from that of husband and wife to one of simply good friends. There was no hint of infidelity, only of seeking support and companionship elsewhere.

Besides Ira Sankey and Phoebe Knapp, Hugh and Louise Main were good friends of Fanny. On March 24, 1884, they held the first of the annual Fanny Crosby birthday parties that were to become a yearly tradition at the offices of Biglow and Main on Ninth Street and Madison Avenue. After twenty years and some three thousand hymns, Hugh thought Fanny was more than due an annual tribute. A sumptuous table was spread at the office, prepared by the wives of members of the publishing firm. The highlight of the evening was the reading of birthday poems written in her honor by Main, Sankey, Kirkpatrick, Lowry, Doane, and others. Hugh's comic poem so delighted her that it became the highlight of subsequent celebrations.

In October 1884 Moody came to New York to lead, along with Sankey, a "Christian convention" on evangelism. They held meetings at the Lafayette Avenue Presbyterian Church in Brooklyn, a short distance from Sankey's home. Moody was concerned about the personal evangelism of church members. If there were to be a meaningful revival, laymen had to do their part. So Moody suggested individual churches hold revivals at regular intervals.

Fanny continued to write hymns for Sankey and for Biglow and Main. She was writing perhaps her most successful hymns at this time for Kirkpatrick and Sweney. Among the many she contributed to *Songs of Redeeming Love* (1882) and *Glad Hallelujahs* (1887) were "Tell Me the Story of Jesus," "Redeemed, O How I Love to Proclaim It," and "We Are Never Weary of the Grand Old Song." By far the most successful hymn she wrote for them was "He Hideth My Soul in the Cleft of the Rock," for which Kirkie provided the music.

> BY FAR THE MOST SUCCESSFUL HYMN SHE WROTE WAS "HE HIDETH MY SOUL IN THE CLEFT OF THE ROCK."

Fanny continued her work in the missions, although she lost a good friend in Jerry McAuley. The Irishman had never been well, and his labors at the mission put his health under a terrible strain. By his mid-forties, he was suffering from tuberculosis. The end came unexpectedly in October 1884. Sam Hadley took his place as director of the Water Street Mission.

Fanny came to know and admire Sam, but she was better acquainted with his brother, Henry Harrison Hadley, known as the Colonel, who had a distinguished Civil War record. Alcoholism cost him his thriving law practice, and he began publishing a weekly paper in Upper Manhattan, for which Fanny wrote poems espousing temperance. Hadley thought he could learn to drink in moderation, but he was forced to conclude that for people of his type, a "moderation society" was useless. He stayed off the bottle for a while, but in trying to drink socially he had become addicted again and by the summer of 1886 was taking more than forty drinks a day.

Fanny tried her best to counsel the Colonel, who was a nominal Anglican but held "original ideas on religion." He finally was converted after hearing the testimony of a recovered alcoholic at his brother's mission. Hadley prayed to God not to remove his "appetite for drink" but to enable him to bear "this thirst" as long as he lived, in gratitude for Christ dying for him on the cross. He awoke the next morning singing. He no longer felt a desire for strong drink or tobacco.

Before he died sixteen years later, Hadley had founded sixty rescue missions and became an internationally known Christian lecturer.

Fanny was overjoyed in the summer and autumn of 1886 not only by the conversion of her editor friend but by the things she had seen happening in Northfield, Massachusetts. In 1879, D. L. Moody had held the first of the Northfield Christian Workers' Conferences that would become an annual affair in his hometown. Moody liked to spend the summer in study and relaxation at Northfield, where he owned a fine home. He could not relax for long, however, and soon he was conducting public Bible readings in his dining room, inviting everyone in the area who was interested. There were so many people, they could not get into the house; the porch was crowded with people looking through the window.

Encouraged by the show of interest, Moody decided it might be a good idea for Christian workers to meet for a week each summer in that rustic paradise, to pray and study scripture and find greater strength to perform their service in Christian work.

Three hundred people attended the first retreat in September 1879. Housed in the Northfield Seminary dormitory, they met for ten days, studying "the doctrine of the Holy Spirit" and praying for various Christian institutions.

Fanny had heard of the meetings since their inception, but it was not until 1886 that she attended. She stayed with the Sankeys at their summer home in Northfield. She was very pleased with the meetings, held in tents and in the seminary chapel. Moody wanted her to speak from time to time, but she always refused. Nor would she speak at Ocean Grove. Undoubtedly, she came to the retreats as a recipient rather than a dispenser of religious instruction. These were her vacations, her only respites from the constant round of talks and addresses she was obliged to give during the year.

She did compose a few hymns there, however. Vacation or not, she could not resist the promptings of the Holy Ghost.

That fall, her rest over, she returned from the "mountain air so sweet" to New York's foul atmosphere. She was happily at work on her hymns, as usual—and on a sentimental operetta, *Zanie*, which would be produced the following year. Fanny had been engaged as librettist by Hart Pease Danks (1834–1903), a well-known composer of secular music, famous for his hit song "Silver Threads Among the Gold."

Unlike many of her contemporaries, Fanny was not opposed to the theater. Moody and Sankey would never attend, but Fanny felt that as long as the content was wholesome and edifying, there was nothing wrong with a play or opera or

UNLIKE MANY OF HER CONTEMPORARIES, FANNY WAS NOT OPPOSED TO THE THEATER.

popular music. The year after *Zanie*, she collaborated with Howard

Doane in writing a totally secular Christmas cantata titled "Santa Claus." An introduction explained that "this cantata has a religious sentiment pervading it, intending to illustrate the triumph of Right over Wrong."

Fanny was very concerned with her family. Her sister, Carrie, in Bridgeport was again a widow; her husband, Lee Rider, an epileptic, had died in December 1883 at thirty-six. Carrie worked out her grief by providing a home for her aged mother, who still lived with her.

Fanny now was more concerned with Jule and Byron. Byron's health was failing. Despite a weakening heart, in the spring of 1887, he took a job in New Haven, Connecticut, and forced himself to commute about fifty miles each day on the train. It proved to be too much. In the fall he had to give it up; he died in December at age fifty.

Fanny felt the loss of her brothers-in-law keenly, for she was very fond of them both.

Within a month of Byron's death, she lost her one surviving aunt, Polly Decker, to a heart attack at seventy. Polly was just two years Fanny's senior and had been more of a sister than an aunt during their childhood. Until she was five, Fanny had been Polly's constant playmate. One of the last links to her childhood was broken forever. From those long-vanished days in Gayville, only one figure remained: "Mother Dear," still hale and hearty at eighty-eight.

In March 1889, Grover Cleveland completed his term as president of the United States and moved to a home on Madison Avenue in New York. Soon afterward, he invited Fanny to come see him. Thus, after an interval of thirty-five years, a friendship begun at the New York Institution for the Blind was renewed. At their reunion, she was received kindly by her old friend, grown bald and jowly, and by his beautiful young wife, Frankie. Cleveland insisted they regularly keep in touch.

In 1889, Fanny contributed forty hymns to Lowry and Doane's *Bright Array*, but none achieved any degree of popularity. She was now almost totally written out. Everything she produced was probably the fifth or sixth paraphrase of something she had written years before. The quality of her hymns was deteriorating. But Biglow and Main wanted more and more hymns, and Fanny supplied them. They even insisted she write paraphrases of popular hymns by other authors, such as "Wonderful Words of Life" (Bliss) and "Showers of Blessing" (Whittle). But her versions were quickly forgotten.

Fanny wrote so many hymns, most of them rapidly and mechanically, that she often could not remember what she had written. She sometimes could not even recognize her own hymns when they were sung.

She would write perhaps no more than a half-dozen good hymns in the next quarter-century, but her fame continued to grow immensely because of her past achievements and her reputation as a preacher and lecturer. Her most effective contributions

> HER MOST EFFECTIVE CONTRIBUTIONS IN THE FUTURE WOULD BE FROM THE PULPIT OR LECTERN.

in the future would be from the pulpit or lectern, but she was always known as "the hymn writer" and "the queen of gospel song."

17
HER LAST GREAT HYMN

The same month Fanny celebrated her seventieth birthday, Moody came back to New York for his first major campaign since 1876. The decade-and-a-half since he and Sankey had taken New York by storm had produced many changes. Always thickset, Moody had grown stupendously fat. He was so stout he had to have clothes specially made and either wear loafers or have one of his sons tie his shoes. With his enormous white beard and ruddy complexion, he looked remarkably like Santa Claus.

Time had altered not only Moody's appearance but also his audiences. He no longer had to engage the largest halls, for his middle-aged and elderly listeners could be accommodated at local churches. The fact that most people who attended already were "saved" disappointed the evangelist. He complained bitterly that his meetings were attended only by "chronic attenders of religious meetings, who crowd everybody else out." He groused that he seemed to be looking at the same faces that had greeted him a decade before.

Sankey did not accompany Moody this time. Although he was not yet fifty, the baritone's once-golden voice was now almost completely a thing of the past, and he sang only occasionally. Tenor George Stebbins served as soloist and song leader.

In the "Bible readings," as he called his meetings, Moody spoke of the declining interest of religion in America. The revival that had begun in the 1850s and peaked in the 1870s had completely run its course, and Moody was very concerned. He wondered how religion could be made more palatable to the young. From the pulpit of the Marble Collegiate Church in 1890, he urged ministers to give shorter sermons and inject greater pep into their services. Clergymen, he said, should not take for themselves the pretentious title "Reverend," for that was reserved for Christ; a minister should be content with "Mister" like any other man.

Fanny attended but predictably refused all Moody's requests to speak or even appear on the platform. At one of the meetings, however, Fanny was unable to find a seat in the crowded church. She was about to leave when Moody's son Will told her he would find her a seat. The people were singing "Blessed Assurance" as he led her into the chancel and onto the platform. The evangelist stood up and raised his hand to interrupt the singing. "Praise the Lord, here comes the authoress!" he shouted. It was too late for Fanny to avoid a seat on the platform, and she sat amid a thunderous ovation. She took the incident in good humor.

> "PRAISE THE LORD, HERE COMES THE AUTHORESS!" HE SHOUTED.

May brought her to Bridgeport, and on the thirtieth, she addressed a Decoration Day crowd in Seaside Park, reciting a poem written for the local post of the Grand Army of the Republic. The appearance was such a success, she was invited to make it an annual event. For the rest of her life, the Decoration Day poem and address would be an institution in Bridgeport. At ninety, she still could move aging veterans and their families to tears.

The following day, Fanny helped her mother celebrate her ninety-first birthday. Mercy's birthday was always the high point of the year for her adoring family. Mercy, who lived with Carrie in an apartment on Washington Avenue, was still apparently in good health and in full possession of her faculties. She was joined by a large host of relatives.

That summer Mercy became painfully ill and was taken to a hospital, where her condition was pronounced hopeless. At sunset on September 1, with Fanny, Carrie, and Jule at her bedside, Mercy "passed peacefully from this world to the brighter home above."

More than the passing of her mother, Fanny was saddened by the conduct of her sisters. Mercy, who had come to Bridgeport a half-century before with nothing, had "a little something" when she died but left no will. Jule and Carrie applied for the estate, declaring themselves the "only heirs and next of kin." Even if she knew, Fanny did not object, and the courts awarded the two sisters Mercy's entire estate. Fanny accepted this without bitterness. She felt God provided for her needs, and that was enough.

The next year, Fanny again found her Muse and wrote two hymns that achieved great success. Early that year, Sweney asked her to write "something tender and pathetic." He proposed, however, a tune that sounded anything but tender and pathetic. It was a peppy, brass bandish piece that sounded very much like "She'll Be Comin' Round the Mountain."

Fanny prayed for the appropriate lyrics. Finally, she entered a "train of thought" that resulted in "My Saviour First of All." Within a few years, almost everyone in England and America knew it.

An even more popular hymn was born shortly thereafter. In March 1891, Fanny's cousin Howard Crosby, the Presbyterian pastor, died of pneumonia at sixty-five. Not long afterward, Lucius Biglow read her a pamphlet containing the text of Dr. Crosby's last message. It said no Christian need fear death. "If each of us is faithful to the grace which is given us by Christ, that same grace which teaches us how to live will also teach us how to die."

Moved by that last message, Fanny wrote a poem called "Some Day." It was written in a matter of minutes under "divine inspiration," as she had written her best hymns of the sixties and seventies. She put it in the hands of Biglow, who paid her the usual two dollars and put it in his vault. For three years, "Some Day" seemed

> HER "HEART'S SONG" WAS TO BECOME THE WELL-KNOWN "SAVED BY GRACE."

destined to be one of those poems Fanny considered among her better efforts but not set to music. But with slight variations, this poem—her "heart's song"—was to become the well-known "Saved by Grace."

Fanny had good reason to reflect on death that year. First, her mother had died, then her cousin, Howard. In July, she received word from Bridgeport that "the White-Robed Angel" had taken her favorite grandniece, Clare Morris, after a bout with scarlet fever. Fanny had not fully recovered from that blow when in September she learned Joseph Knapp had died suddenly aboard ship while returning with Phoebe from a European vacation.

Despite grief and trouble, Fanny was blessed with several excellent friends. There were Ira Sankey, Phoebe Knapp, and Howard Doane. Now, in the 1890s, she began two more great friendships.

At Cornell Methodist Church, she developed a close friendship with the assistant pastor, Rev. Gerhard Johannes Schilling. A native of Germany, Schilling was converted in Burma—a conversion that cost him his job—and came to New York, where he entered divinity school. Forty years her junior, Schilling picked up "Aunt Fanny" in his carriage every Sunday and Wednesday evening for church. He came to know and love her hymns. In 1894, with his American wife, Schilling left for the mission field in Burma, where he translated the Bible and wrote hymns in the native dialect. He claimed Fanny as his inspiration.

Fanny also came to know Eliza Edmunds Hewitt. Born in Philadelphia in 1851, Eliza—sometimes called Lida—had taught for a few years until she was stricken with a painful, incapacitating disease of the spinal cord. After several years in bed, she regained enough strength to become an active church worker. She began to write religious poems that attracted the attention of William Kirkpatrick, who, along with Sweney, set some of them to music. As the years went by, Eliza supplied fifteen hundred hymns for Kirkpatrick and Sweney. By the mid-nineties, she was one of the grand duchesses in the court of Fanny Crosby, the acknowledged queen of the gospel hymn.

In 1894, Stebbins was given the opportunity to set Fanny's "heart's song" to music. Fanny was spending the summer with the Sankeys in Northfield, Massachusetts. The Moodys were in Europe that summer, and the Northfield Bible conference was headed by Dr. Adoniram Judson Gordon, an eminent Baptist clergyman and writer. One of his lectures was on the subject of the Holy Spirit. After his address, Sankey came to Fanny and asked, "Will you say something? There is a request from the audience that you speak."

"Oh, Sankey, I cannot speak before such an array of talent!"

Gordon then added, "Fanny, do you speak to please man or to please God?"

That pricked her conscience. "Why, I hope to please God!"

"Well, then," said Gordon, "go out and do your duty."

Taking her position at the lectern, Fanny made a few remarks, then quoted her "heart's song," the poem "Some Day." It began:

Some day my earthly house will fall,
I cannot tell how soon 'twill be,
But this I know, my All in All
Has now a place in heaven for me.

When she had finished, there was not a dry eye in the auditorium.

Sankey sent the poem to Stebbins, who had Fanny provide a chorus:

And I shall see Him face to face,
And tell the story—Saved by Grace.

He set it to a slow tune. Although the music is not particularly delicate or melodic, Fanny's "heart's song" became a favorite among evangelical Christians the world over. Moody loved it as soon as he heard it. A hit song of the Gay Nineties, it was on everybody's lips.

It was to be Fanny's last truly popular hymn.

> FANNY'S "HEART'S SONG" BECAME A FAVORITE AMONG EVANGELICAL CHRISTIANS THE WORLD OVER.

18
OLD, POOR, BUT POPULAR

In the 1890s, the worn little woman who was the queen of the gospel song was a familiar figure along Manhattan's streets. She was frequently recognized, perpetually smiling—as much as her ill-fitting dentures would permit her—and clinging to the hand of a companion. By now, she was quite bent and stooped and wore a curly brown wig over her thin gray hair. The style of her gowns and bonnets was of the 1840s. But her energy, verve, mental acuity, enjoyment of life, and sense of humor did not seem to be that of a woman of seventy-five. Despite her ravaged form, Fanny seriously contended she felt no different than she had at sixteen.

She kept up a round of activity that would have exhausted many a person forty years younger. She still provided Biglow and Main with two or three hymns a week and wrote for Sweney and Kirkpatrick. She still worked tirelessly at reforming the drunkards, dope fiends, and derelicts at the Bowery, Water Street, and Cremorne missions and at the Door of Hope. Her time was constantly booked for speeches and lectures for the Railroad Branch of the YMCA and at churches and grange halls in various towns and cities. During spare moments, she did not rock by the fire but engaged in intellectually stimulating conversation or music with Sankey, Phoebe, and other friends. When she talked, she usually was knitting or sewing, too, for she was nervous if her hands were not constantly occupied.

SHE WAS NERVOUS IF HER HANDS WERE NOT CONSTANTLY OCCUPIED.

In 1896, Fanny moved to Brooklyn, taking a room alone in a poor section of town on Lafayette Avenue. She was not far from the Sankeys and Stebbinses, who regularly looked in on her. Van was now boarding with his friends, the Underhills, in a fashionable apartment on South Third Street in Brooklyn. Fanny frequently called on this "good friend."

D. L. Moody arrived in Manhattan to win more of the unbelieving to Christ. Christian workers were beginning to realize there were just as many heathen on the streets of New York and Washington as there were on those of Timbuktu or Calcutta, and Moody promised his biggest campaign since 1876. But the almost rabid religious fervor that had characterized the late 1850s and the next two decades had subsided in the '80s. As the twentieth century approached, the masses were lukewarm toward religion. It was the "Gilded Age" when many devoted their lives to building fortunes. At the same time, increasing numbers of discontented poor were finding their solace not in religion, as their ancestors had, but in socialism, communism, and anarchism.

Moody was welcomed with only a shadow of the enthusiasm that had greeted him in 1876. One well-known minister maintained there was no evidence that Moody's past campaigns had made any substantial or permanent increase in church attendance and expressed doubts whether the projected November campaign would be helpful or desirable for the local churches. Others believed a revival in the New York area was desperately needed, but they questioned whether a Moody revival would fill the bill.

On November 8, the grizzled evangelist opened his campaign in the Carnegie Music Hall. He had intended to "speak to the unconverted," but as he addressed the typical middle-aged, churchy audience he had deplored in his 1890 "Bible readings," he changed his mind. After making it perfectly clear that his hearers were more diligent in their worldly business than in their Christian faith, he lambasted his hearers for their lack of social action on a personal level. "Send your carriage out and give poor people a drive in the park once in a while, and they'll call you an angel, I'll warrant." Moody was not so much concerned with working to solve the evils of society as with individuals. Society could not be changed until individuals were.

In the next few days, Moody moved out into the local churches. He wanted these congregations to act as "fire-centers from which to spread the flames" of revival. He had come to realize that at least in big cities he could win few to Christ through mass meetings. The giant auditoriums rented by his supporters were filled largely with people who were already Christian, not the indifferent or the "infidels" he wanted to reach. But he was convinced every man and woman in New York City could be reached if he could get the cooperation of local pastors and congregations. He wanted the pastors to witness house to house. He wanted pastors and people to hold small, intimate, neighborhood "cottage meetings" for prayer, discussion, and devotion.

The parishioners would not go out to encourage their unchurched friends to come, but they flocked to hear Moody at his first "fire-center" meeting at the Marble Collegiate Church.

Sankey was with his old friend this time, but his charm had faded considerably. He was described by one observer as "an immense, bilious man with eyes surrounded by flaccid, pendent, baggy wrinkles." His gestures were "unctuous," and he rolled his eyes "in an affected manner" as he sang in a ravaged voice.

Moody moved the meetings to Cooper Union, an educational institution in downtown Manhattan in whose Great Hall he undertook another series of mass meetings. Here he thundered against the "higher criticism" of the Bible, through which many pages of scripture were being dismissed as spurious or explained away as myth or legend.

For Moody, things went from bad to worse. After several mass meetings at Cooper Union, he carried the campaign to an old brownstone church on Fourteenth Street and Second Avenue. The church was virtually empty as he lumbered onto the platform for the first address.

"Where are the people?" he asked, bewildered.

The pastor of the church shrugged his shoulders and said drily, "On the streets."

Moody was angered, feeling the pastor had not done his part in trying to recruit an audience. "Well," he roared, "why don't you go out and get them?"

He held up the service until the minister and several other local clergymen could go out and round up more people. They frantically searched high and low, but nobody seemed interested. Finally, two of them entered a bar. To the men who stood about, they asked sheepishly, "Don't you want to come to the church on the corner of Second Avenue and hear Dwight L. Moody preach?"

"Who is Moody?" growled one of the men, who went on drinking with his companions.

Moody had to admit "complete defeat" in his 1896 campaign to bring the Gospel to New York City. Like many of his friends who ran the rescue missions, he must have felt that somehow he was losing his grip on the masses.

Fanny's hymn "Saved by Grace" became a consolation to the old man. He had it sung at nearly every service, sometimes three times a night. As it was sung, the preacher would sit with a far-off look in his eyes while tears ran down his red cheeks.

It was during this time that Dr. Lowry, white-bearded and deaf, decided to do something to secure an income for Fanny's closing years. The demand for hymns and hymnals was diminishing. He and Doane were working on what would prove to be their last effort, *The Royal Hymnal*. The good doctor anticipated that in the coming years, Fanny would have considerably less work and less income. As it was, she never earned more than four hundred dollars a year— a small sum even for that time.

> SHE NEVER EARNED MORE THAN FOUR HUNDRED DOLLARS A YEAR—A SMALL SUM EVEN FOR THAT TIME.

So Lowry decided to have Fanny publish another collection of poems, *Bells at Evening*. In addition to an excellent biographical sketch written by Lowry, it included poems from Fanny's three earlier volumes, now long since out of print. There were also secular poems and what Fanny considered to be the best of her hymns. *Bells at Evening*, with 224 pages, sold at fifty cents a copy, and Biglow and Main saw to it that all the profit went to Fanny. The volume sold nicely, and there were several editions.

Some felt Fanny still was not sufficiently remunerated for her great work. Many thought she should be well-to-do, as were many of her peers. Moody owned a fine house in Northfield, Sankey a fine house in Brooklyn and a summer home in Northfield. Why shouldn't Fanny be as well off as her friends?

Phoebe Knapp, probably her richest friend, was especially determined to do something. Unable to persuade Fanny to accept monetary gifts, she approached the poet Will Carleton (1845–1912), author of many volumes of popular sentimental verse and editor of the magazine *Every Where*. He had known Fanny for several years and loved and admired her. Phoebe suggested he take down from Fanny's dictation the story of her early life and publish it in serial form in *Every Where*, which Carleton consented to do. Part of the profit from the articles would go to Fanny, and her financial situation could improve without her feeling she was receiving charity.

Carleton was appalled by the conditions in which the world-beloved hymn writer was living. While she was "not in actual want," her one-room dwelling in a poor Brooklyn neighborhood was not, he believed, worthy of someone with her reputation.

Carleton drew from her "detached narratives" an account of her life story. He wrote the articles, secured her approval, and published them in *Every Where* over a period of months, paying her ten dollars for each article.

Hugh Main, Howard Doane, and others in the firm of Biglow and Main were offended because Carleton implied and Phoebe Knapp insisted they were not paying Fanny enough. Indignantly, they pointed out that Fanny was receiving far more from *Bells at Evening* than from Carleton's articles. Justifiably, they pointed out that far from helping Fanny financially, Carleton was hurting her by providing competition and cutting down the sales of a book whose profits would benefit her far more than would the articles.

This was the beginning of a quarrel between Doane and Main and Carleton and Phoebe that would reach a climax within a few years. No one seemed to realize Fanny was poor by choice. Although

> NO ONE SEEMED TO REALIZE FANNY WAS POOR BY CHOICE.

she appreciated the efforts of these friends in her behalf, Fanny did not want to be wealthy. She could have insisted Biglow and Main pay a higher fee; many hymn writers less celebrated than she charged up to ten dollars for their efforts. But she settled for the minimum and never set a price for her services as a speaker, often refusing honoraria. When forced to accept money, she always protested she was being given too much. She gave away practically all she received and prayed for food, rent, or whatever she needed from day to day.

Moody proposed to Main that instead of paying Fanny two dollars for each hymn, he pay her a regular weekly salary of eight dollars. Main consented. This brought in $416 a year, roughly the equivalent of what she had been receiving by being paid for each hymn. But Moody and Main knew in coming years there would be fewer hymns published, and this new arrangement would ensure that Fanny received a steady income, even though she would be asked to write fewer hymns.

Fanny's friends had good reason for their anxiety. She was close to eighty, and she looked terrible. The fact that she persisted in living alone worried both friends and family. The sisters in Bridgeport urged her to come north and make her home with them, but Fanny refused.

Once during this period, in Northfield, she fell down the steps of Moody's house and was seriously cut. Shortly after recovering, she suffered a heart attack in Brooklyn, and for a while her life hung in the balance. For days she was in a partial coma. She made a complete recovery but refused the urgings of her friends and doctors to rest.

Fanny resumed her former work in the New York night missions as soon as she could. She also continued to travel and lecture in New England, insisting she needed no companion. In the summer of 1897, she revisited the scenes of her childhood—perhaps for the first time since she had left to attend the Institution for the Blind. Invited to address the graduating women of Drew Seminary in Carmel, near Gayville, she delighted the audience with reminiscences about the locality in the days of her youth.

In August, she journeyed once more to central New York. Named poet laureate of the Chautauqua Circle at Tully Lake, she had consented to attend their summer Round Table and deliver at least one major poetic address. At Assembly Park at Tully Lake near Syracuse, one of about a hundred Chautauqua centers thriving at the time, audiences were instructed and entertained by speakers and performers from diverse fields. There might be a reading from *Hamlet,* a lecture by a Syracuse doctor on the eye, a lecture by a local woman on her recent trip to Japan, and a solo by a local tenor. Fanny, a nationally known poet, was the star attraction.

Amazingly, in addition to her daily recitations, she fulfilled speaking engagements at nearby places such as a rescue mission, state fair, Indian reservation, the Elmwood Grange, a home for the elderly, and a church.

Somehow she found time for relaxation at Tully Lake. Eliza Hewitt annually attended the Round Table and was her companion there. Here Fanny enjoyed the friendship of a woman who was almost like a sister to her.

Fanny was never too busy to receive "pilgrims" who came to call. Her hosts, the John Roberts family in Tully, realized she needed time to prepare her poems and addresses, so they tried to shoo away the callers who constantly sought her out during the

FANNY WAS NEVER TOO BUSY TO RECEIVE "PILGRIMS" WHO CAME TO CALL.

evenings. But Fanny would not hear of it! She would interrupt whatever she was doing to spend time with her callers.

In January 1898, Moody returned to New York for a two-month campaign. His meetings at Carnegie Hall were not so much for converting unbelievers as for enlightening and empowering those who were already faithful. He had concluded that it was the individual Christian who had to be the evangelist in the modern city, witnessing to unbelievers who were neighbors or coworkers.

Moody was sixty-one and looked older than seventy, unwieldy and dropsical, moving with difficulty, often gasping for breath. He spoke much about death.

At first, the meetings were attended heavily, chiefly by elderly women who "sobbed convulsively" during the service. Sankey did not appear. The music leadership was divided between Victor Benke, the young organist of the Bowery Mission; J. H. Burke, a Chicago soloist; and stout, gray, ailing John Sweney.

The campaign closed March 20, and Moody looked terribly weary. After a good beginning, his crowds had dwindled to a nearly empty hall. In May and August, he returned to speak in the New York area, raising funds for evangelical work among soldiers preparing to leave for the Spanish-American War. His efforts met with little success.

While the popularity of other celebrities in the religious world of her generation declined, Fanny's grew. This perhaps owed to the fact that she spoke to small groups and came across better as a personality than preachers like Moody and Whittle, who appeared amid a sea of humanity in cavernous auditoriums. It also may have owed to her positive approach. The typical nineteenth-century preacher chided, scolded, and threatened; Fanny, assuming her audience already knew they were sinners, offered messages of comfort and encouragement.

Then, too, she possessed something special that could draw the unchurched to meetings: her blindness. And, of course, much of Fanny's appeal stemmed from her charisma and indefinable mystique that overwhelmed all who met her. Even those who bitterly criticized the quality of her hymns had to admit that as a person she had an irresistible charm and indisputable holiness.

19
WIDOWED

The generation of hymn tune composers who had helped Fanny create her greatest hits were beginning to pass from the scene. Chester Allen, Silas Vail, and William Sherwin were already dead. John Sweney suffered a stroke shortly after the Moody campaign and died in April 1899. Next it was Lowry's turn to rest. His health had been in decline, and Fanny went to Plainfield, New Jersey, to visit him at home, where he was bedfast and in pain. They reminisced about events of the past years. Finally, the dying man turned the conversation to the thing that most concerned him: his approaching death.

Fanny," he whispered softly, "I am going to join those who have gone before. My work is now done."

Fanny, with a lump growing in her throat, found herself unable to speak without betraying her grief. "So I simply took his hand in mine and said quietly, 'I thank you, Dr. Lowry, for all that you have done for me.' "Then, echoing the words of the hymn they had written together years before, she said, "Good night, until we meet in the morning." Lowry died November 25.

A new generation of hymn writers was rising. Some of them composed in a style identical to that of their predecessors. Charles Hutchison Gabriel of Iowa was probably the hymn writer who most aptly can be called the successor to Lowry, Doane, Sankey,

Sweney, and Kirkpatrick. His hymns were very simple and had "the old Methodist swing." Completely self-taught, he of-

A NEW GENERATION OF HYMN WRITERS WAS RISING.

ten wrote his own words, attributing the lyrics to "Charlotte G. Homer" and other pen names.

Inevitably, Fanny was asked to supply Gabriel with hymns, which she did increasingly as the years went by. Among those for which Gabriel supplied the tunes were "Hold Fast," "Lead Me, My Saviour," and "Sunshine on the Hill." Like most of her hymns of this period, the lyrics she provided for Gabriel were essentially repeats of her previous works, paraphrased for the fifteenth or twentieth time.

She worked with several other younger musicians. Adam Geibel, born in Germany, like Fanny was blinded at an early age by inept treatment of an eye infection. Mary Upham, a distant cousin of Fanny's, had been a well-known concert singer before she decided, for religious reasons, to give up singing all secular music. Victor Benke, also born in Germany, was the organist at the Bowery Mission.

The most accomplished and successful of Fanny's younger collaborators was Ira Allan Sankey, third and youngest son of her great friend. Born in Edinburgh, Scotland, in 1874 during his father's first overseas campaign, young Sankey from early childhood showed "an intense love for the arts, especially music." At Princeton University, he studied to be an architect and civil engineer, but after his graduation in 1897, he could not resist the lure of his first love, and he went to work for Biglow and Main. His superior talent was recognized at once by his father and colleagues, and Allan was soon composing a large number of the tunes for the firm.

Fanny had known Allan from the time he was a baby and watched with great interest his progress as a composer. Of all the men for whom she ever wrote, Allan was the one whose musicianship Fanny praised without reservation. She wrote that young Sankey's music was "unusually sweet and beautiful." As much as she loved Ira Sankey as a person, she said, "the son surpassed the father in sweetness of tone and harmony of expression."

They began to collaborate in 1899, and their work together continued until their deaths sixteen years later. More than any other gospel hymn tune writer, Allan could express the emotional power of Fanny's poems. He set to music some of her more complicated hymns, such as "God's Peace I'll Know." They were more beautiful to listen to than the tunes of Doane and Lowry, and they were more difficult to sing and play on the piano or organ.

> **MORE THAN ANY OTHER GOSPEL HYMN TUNE WRITER, ALLAN COULD EXPRESS THE EMOTIONAL POWER OF FANNY'S POEMS.**

Their most popular hymn was "Never Give Up," for which Allan wrote a simple, straightforward tune in the old style.

Never be sad or desponding,
If thou hath faith to believe,
Grace, for the duties before thee
Ask of thy God and receive.

Never give up, never give up,
Never give up to thy sorrows,
Jesus will bid them depart,
Trust in the Lord, trust in the Lord,
Sing when your trials are greatest,
Trust in the Lord and take heart!

Fanny considered it one of her most effective poems. It became popular in the early 1900s, when it was a favorite with the British evangelist Rodney "Gipsy" Smith (1860–1947).

Allan Sankey was also vice-president of the Leeds and Catlin Phonograph Company, and through his efforts some of the leading lights of the Moody-Sankey years were persuaded to record their voices for posterity. The elder Sankey preserved on wax the pathetic remains of his once-glorious voice with his famous "The Ninety and Nine" and several other hymns. Moody was induced to make at least one recording, reciting the Beatitudes. Stebbins, Sam Hadley, and others were recorded singing hymns. There is no evidence Fanny ever had her voice recorded.

In November Moody traveled west to conduct a campaign in Kansas City. Nearly forty years of his grueling routine had aged him prematurely. He had suffered a heart condition for several years, and now he was in constant pain. Flushed in the face, he breathed with difficulty. His frame, already corpulent, was swollen with dropsy to immense proportions. He was scarcely able to walk; the slightest exertion left him exhausted.

Moody was taken back to Northfield by rail and agonized toward death for a month. Joy came on the morning of December 22.

Back in Brooklyn, Fanny pondered what manner of man her revered Moody had been. To a reporter some years later, Fanny said of her friend, "I have never known a kinder, bigger-hearted man than Dwight L. Moody. His work was a miracle and a constant inspiration through all my work. His influence was the light—sanative and bracing."

Fanny continued to write hymns, travel, preach, and work in the night missions until spring, when shortly after her eightieth birthday, the inevitable collapse came. She fell ill with bronchial

SHORTLY AFTER HER EIGHTIETH BIRTHDAY, THE INEVITABLE COLLAPSE CAME. pneumonia. For the second time in four years, she was "almost in sight of the harbor." But her remarkable constitution pulled her through, despite a heart condition.

Carrie and Jule had hurried down to Brooklyn to Fanny's room on Lafayette Avenue when they were informed of their sister's illness. This time they insisted she leave Brooklyn and come with them. Fanny at first objected, but when Hugh Main and the Sankeys seconded Carrie and Jule—and when her sisters agreed she could return to the Empire City for frequent visits—she relented.

In June 1890, she left New York after a residence there of sixty-five years. For the first time since she was fifteen, Fanny was making her home with relatives. Carrie and Fanny ultimately moved into an apartment in a fine brick house owned by William and Sarah Becker on State Street. There they would stay the next six years.

Their rent was paid by Ira Sankey, who also sent Carrie a sum of money each month with which to provide for the needs of the poet. (He knew better than to send it to Fanny, who would always find someone worse off than she and give it away!) This dwelling, in a good section of the city, was by far the most congenial residence Fanny had ever known. The apartment consisted of five large rooms, into which Carrie moved her furniture. It was a pleasant, cozy place. The living room had a bay window in which Fanny loved to sit and rock. The parlor was dominated by an enormous portrait of Mercy, whose memory both sisters fervently loved.

Carolyn Rider was a short, heavyset woman with a long, homely face offset by a lovely smile and twinkling eyes. She has been described as jolly and sweet, especially fond of children. Like her famous sister, she was disarmingly frank, sincere, and confiding, hating pretense and deceit. She was quiet and extremely shy. For the sake of Fanny, she put up with the hurly-burly of public life, devoting her remaining years to being her sister's eyes. "She has sacrificed her life for me," Fanny later said of her.

For the rest of her life, Carrie would serve as Fanny's secretary. She read to her all the mail that arrived at Fanny's "Box 840" in the Bridgeport Post Office and wrote Fanny's dictated replies. Every morning she would take down any hymn or poem "Sister Fan" had composed during the night. Later, Carrie secured the services of a professional secretary, a young woman named Eva G. Cleaveland, who would relieve her of much of the work. But for the time being, Carrie handled what had been the responsibility of two or three professional secretaries in the offices of Biglow and Main.

Carrie was a devout member of the First Baptist Church in Bridgeport. Fanny occasionally went there with her, but being a Methodist, she went more frequently with Jule to First Methodist Church. Although it was four years before she officially transferred her membership, from the start Fanny was active in the church. She became active in the King's Daughters, a charitable organization connected with the church that ran a hospital and provided food, clothes, and coal for the poor.

Fanny also became active in Bridgeport's Christian Union, an institution that served the same purpose as New York's rescue missions. Every night there was a service for as many derelicts and drunkards as could be rounded up for an audience. Several nights a week, when she was in town, Fanny would be the main speaker.

In August, less than two months after she arrived in Bridgeport, Fanny went to Northfield, a sadder, quieter place now that Moody was gone. As usual, she stayed with Ira and Fanny Sankey.

She visited Moody's widow, Emma, and paid a final call on Daniel Whittle, who was dying of an excruciating bone disease.

Fanny spoke to the Northfield conference that year, being led to the lectern by Sankey. When the convention was over, Fanny went to Tully Lake while Sankey set sail for Britain for another campaign. He was in high spirits as he arrived in Ireland, writing Fanny that he had crossed the Atlantic with "no sickness, no sorrow, no sighing." In Belfast, he talked about Fanny so much that a wealthy businessman gave him a present of five pounds in gold for her.

When he returned in January, however, he was completely exhausted and went with his wife to the Kellogg Sanitarium at Battle Creek, Michigan, for a rest. Fanny wrote him a letter in verse:

> *But, oh, a sanitarium fare—*
> *No coffee? Well, I do declare*
> *'Tis rather hard, it seems to me;*
> *But doctors say—and they agree—*
> *The sacrifice is right to make*
> *When ordered for the stomach's sake.*

The Sankeys soon returned from Michigan. But the career of the "Sweet Singer of Israel" was just about at its close. He was remembered, but only as a figure out of the past. It was as if he were already dead. Yet he accepted this and continued the one ministry of which he was still capable: writing hymns. Fanny supplied him with many poems. Among the loveliest of their hymns of this period is "He Who Safely Keepeth."

Fanny also still wrote for Phoebe Knapp. The rich widow, resplendent in silk and satin gowns and diamond tiaras, nearing seventy but with the face and figure of a woman of forty, had decided she and Fanny should publish their future compositions as sheet music. In that way, Fanny would be able to profit financially from her efforts more than she did when her poems were bought and published by a music company. Owning the copyright to the sheet music, she more adequately could benefit from whatever popularity the hymns should attain. Fanny insisted the copyright be Phoebe's property, but the widow made sure the profits went in full to her blind friend.

Fanny still supplied Allan Sankey and Hugh Main with hymns, which they now published not in large hymnals but in collections of six, seven, and eight hymns. Howard Doane, however, was preparing a new full-length hymnal, which he was going to title *Songs of Devotion*. To assist him, Fanny went to his summer home at Watch Hill, Rhode Island, to spend the first part of July.

It was at Doane's home that Fanny received a telegram announcing Van's death. Her husband, whom she continued to visit and with whom she still maintained amicable relations, had been ill with cancer more than a year and in the final month

FANNY RECEIVED A TELEGRAM ANNOUNCING VAN'S DEATH.

had suffered a paralytic shock. The Underhills had faithfully nursed him in this last sickness.

Fanny was heartbroken. Her thoughts went back to that June day nearly a half century before when the "voice of love" first spoke within their breasts and "all the world was changed," when they "were no longer blind, for the light of love showed us where the lilies bloomed, and where the crystal waters find the moss-mantled spring." Although they had not been together for years, in a way they loved each other to the end.

20
FANNY CROSBY DAY

Fanny was away as much as she was home. Whenever she was in Bridgeport, she held open house on Thursdays, which meant anyone could come and talk with the celebrated hymn writer. The rest of her time was spent working with the King's Daughters and at the Christian Union. Even in her eighties, Fanny found little time to rest. Resting was for old people, and she was young, she said.

Fanny had one of the most gratifying experiences of her life in November 1903. She was in Lynn, Massachusetts, speaking at the YMCA, and as usual she recounted stories of how she came to write some of her hymns. On this occasion, she told how "Rescue the Perishing" was inspired by the conversion of a young working man who rejoiced, "Now I can meet my mother in heaven, for now I have found her God!"

After the meeting, several people came to shake hands with her. Among them was a man whose voice did more shaking than his hand. Fanny was dumbfounded when he proclaimed, "Miss Crosby, *I* was that boy who told you more than thirty-five years ago that I had wandered from my mother's God. That evening you spoke, I sought and found peace, and I have tried to live a consistent Christian life ever since. If we never meet again on earth, we will meet up yonder."

He left without giving his name. Fanny was deeply moved by

this "nameless friend who touched a deep chord of sympathy in my heart."

In January, Fanny, accompanied by her niece, Ida Leschon, set out on a grueling speaking tour by train. They journeyed first to Philadelphia, where Fanny held a series of evangelical meetings. Traveling north, they went to Albany, New York, and then to Rochester. Fanny was now a national celebrity at the pinnacle of her fame. A Rochester newspaper observed there was scarcely a religious service in the United States where at least one of her hymns was not sung.

One thing that struck those who saw and heard the blind speaker was her youthful manner. Her face and form betrayed her age, but her voice, mind, and movements were those of a woman in her prime. Reporters claimed "Madame Crosby" could have passed for twenty years younger than her actual age.

> **"MADAME CROSBY" COULD HAVE PASSED FOR TWENTY YEARS YOUNGER THAN HER ACTUAL AGE.**

Fanny and Ida were back in Bridgeport for only a few days before it was time to go to New York. February 2, the fortieth anniversary of her association with Biglow and Main, was to be the occasion of a special celebration in the firm. Many of her old friends and colleagues were present at the banquet prepared by Louise Main and Fanny Sankey. There were Doane, the jolly old "professor" Kirkpatrick, and George Stebbins. Many others assembled to honor the poet who more than anyone else had helped make Biglow and Main one of the leading publishers of church music in the English-speaking world. Fanny was presented with a golden brooch studded with pearls.

Although many complained that the firm had overworked Fanny, she had been glad to do the low-paying work, even at the expense of her talent for writing truly good poetry. It was a work she did for the Lord, and she thanked her friends for "forty years of blessings, peace and tranquillity, like the dew of Hermon and the dew on the mountains of Zion."

Two of Fanny's good friends were absent, and one was her hostess in New York. During trips to the Empire City, Fanny apparently was always put up at the Hotel Savoy by Phoebe Knapp. Phoebe was on the outs with Hugh Main because of Carleton's publications in the late nineties. Now she had made herself all the more *persona non grata* by continually claiming Fanny was underpaid and by enlisting friends in the higher echelons of the Methodist Church to appeal for money for the hymn writer, implying publicly that Fanny was destitute and poorly housed. But since Ira Sankey paid for Fanny and Carrie's accommodations in Bridgeport, and Hugh Main had arranged for her to receive all the royalties from *Bells at Evening*, which was still in print, Fanny's friends at Biglow and Main had grown exceedingly vexed at the conduct of the rich widow.

While at Phoebe's, Fanny worked on several new hymns, which were to be published as sheet music. Phoebe wrote to Carrie, who had inquired when Fanny could be expected back in Bridgeport:

> *I am taking the best care of our dear Fanny—whom we both love. Each time that she comes to me I am so satisfied (and as never before)—that someone in Bridgeport cares for the personal interests of the dear one—and I am happy indeed! . . .I cannot possibly let her go home until Friday next in the afternoon—just now I need her and she is having a good time. Sincerely hoping that you are well. . . .*

Then Phoebe inserted an inexplicable paragraph:

Fanny sends lots of love and says that for just once she is going to try and commence to be good. That is going to be hard work as we all know. For she has been keeping bad company of late and I hear nothing but Mr. Dooly and upon mention of his name she begins a wild dance—and I, awe-stricken, say "shades of night envelope us" and withdraw.

Your friend,
Mrs. J. F. Knapp

Who was Mr. Dooly? What did Phoebe mean when she spoke of Fanny beginning a "wild dance" at the mention of his name? Can she literally have been dancing at her age? No letter or document that has come down to us can shed light upon Fanny and the mysterious Mr. Dooly.

Before she left New York, Fanny called upon her second old friend who was not present at the banquet, Ira Sankey. For more than a year, he had been stone blind, sitting quietly in deep depression at his house in Brooklyn, living with his memories, awaiting death. He was suffering from glaucoma. Surgery was unsuccessful. He instructed his family to deny rumors that he had gone blind; he hoped to recover and did not want to alarm his friends unnecessarily. But as the rumors grew more persistent, his sons Allan and Edward called a press conference the first week in March and confirmed their father had lost his sight.

Fanny, devastated to learn her friend was, like her, bereft of sight, succeeded in improving his spirits somewhat. But he no longer tried to compose tunes, and he appeared no more in public. Sankey spent the rest of his days sitting in his bedroom, lost in memories, or sitting at his harmonium, playing over and over the songs of happier days.

Throughout the spring of 1904, Fanny traveled about, preaching, lecturing, recounting the story of her life. Whenever she was in Bridgeport, she busied herself speaking at the Christian Union, working with the King's Daughters, and receiving the seemingly endless streams of "pilgrims" who descended when she was in town. Although Thursday was her official open house day, she never refused a visitor.

In early June, Fanny and Carrie went west to Buffalo, where she was the major speaker at a Christian Endeavor convention. Despite her advanced years, she spoke three times a day, often to crowds of more than three thousand.

> DESPITE HER ADVANCED YEARS, SHE SPOKE THREE TIMES A DAY, OFTEN TO CROWDS OF MORE THAN THREE THOUSAND.

She not only gave sermons but lectured on mission work and the methods of hymn writing.

In all her appearances in Buffalo, Fanny deeply moved her hearers, but never as many as on the night when, carried away by an impulse, she rose and joined the soloist. A baritone named Jacobs was singing "Saved by Grace," which was still immensely popular. Fanny, scheduled to speak later, sat behind him on the platform. When Jacobs came to the third stanza, Fanny leaped to her feet and began to sing, "Some day, when fades the golden sun. Beneath the rosy-tinted west. . . ." The notes at first seemed "quavering and faltering," as one might expect of an eighty-year-old, and Jacobs lowered his powerful voice so that hers might be heard by the audience. But her voice became higher and stronger as the chorus progressed: "And I shall see Him face to face...." It filled the hall and held the audience spellbound with its beauty and pathos.

It was spontaneous acts like this one, as much as her prepared talks and sermons, that tended to make hearts captive to the little old lady in ancient garb and to the Gospel she proclaimed.

From Buffalo, stopping to lecture at various places along the way, Fanny made her way to Binghamton. People marveled at her vitality. It amazed even Carrie, more than twenty years her sister's junior, who remarked, "She can tire out everyone present, then go home fresh!"

Fanny felt that as long as she kept busy, she would always be "young." She often reiterated that she doubted she would live a year if forced to abandon her work.

> **FANNY FELT THAT AS LONG AS SHE KEPT BUSY, SHE WOULD ALWAYS BE "YOUNG."**

Fanny apparently did not go to Ocean Grove or Northfield that year. Emma Moody was now dead, and with Whittle gone and Sankey confined to his home in Brooklyn, the Bible conferences had lost their appeal to her. She did go to Tully Lake, however, where she participated in the Round Table. She also made her annual visit to the Indian reservation. This year, she and Eliza Hewitt were accorded the great honor of being adopted into the Eel Clan of the Onondaga tribe. Fanny had always been "deeply interested" in the welfare of American Indians, and the adoption into the Onondagas delighted her. Now that she was a "genuine Indian," she began to collect Onondaga folk tales, which she often related in her lectures and sermons.

Fanny also journeyed to East Orange, New Jersey, where she and Carrie visited friends for a week. From there she went to visit

Sankey, address "her men" at the naval YMCA in Brooklyn, and conduct an evangelical meeting for the Y's Railroad Branch in the roundhouse of the Lackawanna Railroad in Hoboken, New Jersey.

Returning to Bridgeport "brown and merry," she was there only long enough to prepare for her autumn travels. Then she was off to New England. At eighty-four, Fanny seemed to have as much energy as Carrie, sixty, and Ida, forty-five. The two younger women had to alternate as her traveling companions.

Fanny always made an effort to be home for two occasions: her mother's birthday and Christmas. She, Carrie, Jule, and Ida still celebrated Mercy's birthday as if she were alive. The sisters and Ida would put a fresh vase of flowers beneath Mercy's huge photograph and set a place at the table for the deceased matriarch. Fanny would recite the poem she still wrote each year in honor of "Mother Dear."

Christmas was a happy occasion. There was a family dinner in which Aunt Fanny would enliven the lulls in conversation with humorous poems composed on the spot. In the afternoon, while the children rested, Fanny made little gifts to be put into the "grab bag" that provided the evening's entertainment. She also made up humorous little poems that were copied and distributed to every family member.

She loved to play with the children. On one occasion, her grand-nephew Ralph Booth begged her to go for a ride on his sled. To the absolute horror of the parents, Aunt Fanny seated herself on the conveyance and let him pull her around the backyard in the snow.

In early March 1905, Fanny and Carrie left for a lecture tour of more than two weeks. On the fifth, she spoke at the YMCA at Fitchburg, Massachusetts, to 750 people packed into a hall built for 650. The audience sang several of her hymns before an area clergyman read a passage of scripture and Fanny stepped forth, holding a little book tight in her hands. She gave no sermon or lecture as such but, as she did so often, told about her life, about how God had enabled her to overcome her handicap and how He had inspired her hymns.

Next she traveled to western New York, where she spoke to a mass meeting of the Railroad YMCA. In Rochester she spoke to the YMCA's Women's Auxiliary and was given a tribute by Mrs. Caroline Atwater Mason (1853–1939), a well-known author of religious novels. After giving an evangelical sermon in a rescue mission, she and Carrie left to journey farther west, stopping at the School for the Blind in Batavia. Then they started back east, addressing the Railroad YMCA in Albany.

On March 24, Fanny would be eighty-five. To honor her, a group of New York clergymen, with the encouragement of Hugh Main and Allan Sankey, decided to hold a Fanny Crosby Sunday in churches on March 26. Adelbert White served as secretary of the Fanny Crosby Day Committee, and Mrs. Ann Cobham, whom Fanny frequently visited in Warren, Pennsylvania, served as assistant. The celebration was publicized nationwide. Dr. Louis Klopsch, editor of the widely circulated *Christian Herald*, advocated that all Christian churches honor the aged hymn writer on the designated Sunday. Her hymns would be used exclusively, and ministers and priests of all denominations would preach on her life as an example of Christian witness. A "love offering" would be taken for her in all the churches where her "day" was observed.

Fanny was nonplused when she learned of the honor, but she made no attempt to stop the plans. "Am I pleased?" she asked rhetorically. "Certainly. Who would not be? Just so long as the celebration in honor of my work is by those who have loved my songs, both the celebration and the contemplated offering will be like the crowning blessing at the close of a long and busy life!" She wanted to make certain God, not she, received the glory.

Fanny Crosby Day was observed not only in America but in England and in such unlikely countries as India and Tasmania.

FANNY CROSBY DAY WAS OBSERVED NOT ONLY IN AMERICA BUT IN ENGLAND.

She received many tributes, including letters from common folk and places she had never visited. A lady from Mississippi sent flowers she had gathered. Grover Cleveland in Princeton commended her "continuous and disinterested labor in uplifting humanity and pointing out the way to an appreciation of God's goodness and mercy."

Fanny attended a reception given by Hugh Main a few days early. On her birthday, she appeared at a reception at the First Methodist Church in Bridgeport. Looking like a "fragile flower," she was led to a special pew draped with an American flag. Suffering from a bad headache, she spoke briefly of her God, "the sunshine of my soul," and warmly thanked her audience for their love, blessing them as she turned to sit down. The choir sang a hymn she had written for the occasion, "O Land of Joy Unseen," set to music by a parishioner, Fred King.

On Sunday, she gave the evening message at the First Baptist Church, Carrie's congregation. The crowd was so huge, it filled not only the large sanctuary but also the Sunday school rooms.

When the festivities were over throughout the nation, she was the recipient of several thousand dollars in love offerings. This time she did not refuse. She was overwhelmed by the display of a nation's love, and her heart was "full" as she rejoiced that "yea, I have a goodly heritage!"

21
MEMORIES OF EIGHTY YEARS

Fanny was on the road again in the autumn of 1905, lecturing in Massachusetts and New Jersey. During the time she found herself at home, she was busily engaged putting the finishing touches on her autobiography, *Memories of Eighty Years*. This seemingly innocuous project had a stormy career beginning several years before.

Because she was an internationally known figure who had lived a long and interesting life, it is understandable that many people had pressed her to write an autobiography. Partial accounts of her life and career had appeared over the years in various magazines and journals. Lowry had written a brief sketch of her life as an introduction to *Bells at Evening*, and two or three years later, Will Carleton's articles had appeared in his *Every Where* magazine. Fanny was so modest, she could not understand why anyone would be interested in her life, but Adelbert White convinced her of a genuine public interest. He offered to help compile the volume, and Carrie also volunteered to help. So in April 1903, Fanny dispatched White to the New York Institution for the Blind for information concerning the years she was there.

Complications rapidly developed. Carleton, knowing the interest of the public in a Fanny Crosby autobiography, told Fanny of his intention to organize his articles about her into book form. He offered her the same royalty he received from Harper's for his own books of poetry, but Fanny told him she was not at all concerned about the royalties and gave him permission to organize the autobiography. She would have preferred to write her own autobiography, but she was reluctant to deny Carleton permission to do with his articles as he wished.

This did not please White and the personnel of Biglow and Main. Not only did her friends feel Fanny should write her own autobiography, they remembered the hard feelings associated with the Carleton articles when they were published and how they had interfered with the sales of *Bells at Evening*. They suspected *Fanny Crosby's Life-Story, by Herself* was simply a moneymaking scheme Carleton was undertaking for his own profit.

Not unexpectedly, Phoebe Knapp became involved. She was not satisfied with anything anyone connected with Biglow and Main had done for Fanny. She enlisted the services of Methodist Bishop Charles Caldwell McCabe (1836–1906), a friend of Phoebe's and Fanny's. Phoebe apparently told him Fanny was destitute. McCabe began to assert publicly that Fanny was in severe financial straits and was "willing to accept financial assistance." McCabe did not consult Fanny except to ask her if she would be willing to accept "a testimonial of [the] love and admiration" of the American people. She could not very well refuse that. She was never told this "testimonial" would be drawn from her admirers' purses based on a "plea of poverty."

McCabe and Phoebe convinced Carleton to circulate a "publisher's advertisement" to accompany *Fanny Crosby's Life-Story*. It gave the impression that poor Aunt Fanny had no place to live and that proceeds from the book would help buy her a home.

Carleton's *Fanny Crosby's Life-Story, by Herself* went over like a lead balloon with Fanny's publishers. The text said nothing unfavorable about them, but neither did it say anything positive about the firm and its members, except that Fanny had cordial, "even affectionate" relations with them. The book dealt primarily with Fanny's early life, before she had become associated with Biglow and Main. Main, Doane, and others indignantly complained they did not receive the recognition they deserved for their part in Fanny's career.

Fanny's friends had more serious reasons for disapproving of Carleton's book. Initially, Carleton had promised Fanny 25 percent of the profits, but for various reasons, he cut the percentage to 10. Most of Fanny's friends felt that if any-one were taking advantage of Fanny, it was not Biglow and

> NEARLY A YEAR AFTER PUBLICATION, *LIFE-STORY* HAD BROUGHT FANNY EXACTLY $285 IN ROYALTIES.

Main—who arranged for the poet to reap all the profits of *Bells at Evening*—but Carleton. They were incensed that nearly a year after publication, *Life-Story* had brought Fanny exactly $285 in royalties.

White and Carrie, in particular, were concerned about the fu-ture of Fanny's own autobiography, which the poet still planned to compile. If she ever got around to writing it, they were going to work out an arrangement similar to that with *Bells at Evening*, in which all the proceeds from the book's sale would go to her. Publication of Carleton's autobiography doubtless would hurt the market for Fanny's own account.

Fanny tried to stay out of the imbroglio, which certainly embar-rassed her. She was not concerned whether she received 10 percent, 25 percent, or nothing at all. According to Carleton's biographer, "with that perfect candor and generosity characteristic of her," she told Carleton "that the articles were his property, as he had written them." Nevertheless, she was concerned because the "autobiography" told little of her life after she became a hymn writer. She felt she owed the public a more accurate and complete picture.

Fanny also disliked the implication that she was kept in poverty by the stinginess of Biglow and Main. If she had ever been in poverty, it was by choice. Now, in Bridgeport, she felt she was living in almost embarrassing luxury because of Sankey's kindness.

In December, White and Doane convinced Fanny to make a public statement in the *Watchman*, a widely circulated religious magazine. She said the Carleton compilation was "not an adequate biography, especially of the last forty years of my life." She decried the published implication "that the book is being sold to raise money to buy me a house."

She sent a letter to the editor of another religious magazine, dealing with the fact that Bishop McCabe had been raising funds for her. While she permitted him to allow for her friends to make her "a testimonial of their love," she never understood that this appeal would be made on "the plea of [her] poverty."

Even Ira Sankey was unable to remain silent. When he learned of "Mrs. Crosby's matter," as Doane had called it, he was so enraged that he made his last public statement in a brief article published in *The Christian* magazine. He implied that the Carleton business had been of satanic origin.

"Mrs. Crosby's matter" came to an end shortly before Fanny Crosby Day in 1905, when Carleton, who had assumed the commotion raised against him was simply the work of "interested friends," realized Fanny herself was offended and stopped lecturing and advertising for the book. In the midst of the controversy, his wife died suddenly, and now it was just as well with him that the matter be dropped. Neither Carleton nor the bishop nor Phoebe had any fraudulent intent but were sincerely motivated to help Fanny—who realized this and remained on good terms with all three until their deaths.

It was during the winter of 1904–1905 that Fanny did most of the work on her autobiography, *Memories of Eighty Years*. She was assisted by

> DURING THE WINTER OF 1904–1905 FANNY DID MOST OF THE WORK ON HER AUTOBIOGRAPHY, *MEMORIES OF EIGHTY YEARS*.

Carrie and Eva Cleaveland, the stenographer, who took down what she dictated, and by Adelbert White, who organized her rambling recollections into a coherent narrative. In the autobiography, she emphasized her hymns and the stories behind them. She recounted cases in which the hymns had helped someone.

Memories of Eighty Years, like so much Fanny did, was written in haste and suffers accordingly. When it went to press in 1906, it was still in many ways rough and disconnected. It praises those whom she had worked with closely during the years. It describes some of her hymn writing and home mission activities, but it is less interesting, less readable, and less finished than Carleton's production. The articles from which Carleton compiled his book had been prepared by Fanny in more relaxed circumstances, under less pressure. So the earlier account in many ways is livelier, wittier, and slightly more coherent.

As with *Bells at Evening,* all the proceeds went to Fanny. Grover Cleveland contributed a written endorsement in the publisher's announcement. The aging Doane, blue-lipped, watery-eyed, and trembling, gave a series of promotional lectures on Fanny, just as Carleton had done to promote *Life-Story*. Even though the overall sales were disappointing to White, they netted Fanny about a thousand dollars.

What with the autobiographies, the donations resulting from lectures by Carleton and Doane, and the love offerings of Fanny

Crosby Day, Aunt Fanny was catapulted, albeit reluctantly, from poverty into something resembling affluence. She never changed her lifestyle; the increased income simply meant she had more to give away. She did save some money, but only so she might provide something for relatives when she died.

AUNT FANNY WAS CATAPULTED, ALBEIT RELUCTANTLY, FROM POVERTY INTO SOMETHING RESEMBLING AFFLUENCE.

Aunt Fanny, as she was now called almost universally, was writing fewer hymns. She had cut back writing from about two hundred hymns a year to about fifty, a quota she was to maintain the rest of her life. Biglow and Main were turning out fewer new hymnals. Most of their hymnals now reproduced hymns from earlier popular collections. In 1903, Fanny had written more than seventy hymns for Funk and Wagnall's *Gloria Deo* collection, but that was the only additional book to which she was asked to contribute.

After the publication of *Memories of Eighty Years*, Fanny's days were filled with concern for "Sister Carrie." In the summer of 1906, Carrie developed intestinal cancer. She failed gradually to the point where she could no longer care for herself nor Fanny for her. Both women were forced to leave the Becker house and stay with their niece, Florence Morris Booth. Florence and Henry Booth and their two nearly grown children lived in a fine house on Wells Street. Carrie died the following June at sixty-three.

Many of her friends feared for Fanny's well-being, knowing how close she had been to her younger sister. Indeed, Fanny was all but crushed by Carrie's death. No sooner had she buried Carrie than she was dealt another blow: Jule's daughter Ida fell ill with intestinal problems and died in September at forty-eight.

Although Fanny felt profoundly the loss of her sister and

niece who had provided her with so much companionship in late years, she resigned herself, saying, "Well, it is God's will, and they are much happier."

22
THEOLOGY

Fanny was to spend the rest of her life with the Booths on Wells Street. Here her niece Florence tried to be the same kind of companion Carrie had been. She has been described as a "tall, slim, pretty woman" with a pleasant disposition. She left business matters entirely to Eva Cleaveland, who came every day and handled all the correspondence and took down all the hymns and poems Fanny composed. In her late years, Fanny traveled less, but at home she did not get much rest, for she was constantly besieged by many visitors, including journalists who made her the subject of numerous newspaper and magazine articles. It is from these years that we get the most comprehensive picture of her thought, personality, and appearance.

THERE WAS A SPIRIT SHINING THROUGH THE DECAYING SHELL THAT MADE HER BEAUTIFUL.

Fanny now was physically little more than a skeleton. But there was a spirit shining through the decaying shell that made her beautiful. Her smile was said to have been lovely, and all reports speak of the great sweetness and beauty of her voice. She spoke with the rural New England accent that omits "r" and pronounces the final "o" as "er," as in "Longfeller" (one of her favorite poets).

For someone so tiny, Aunt Fanny was a remarkably heavy eater. After downing a bowl of hot coffee after she arose at 11 a.m., she would eat a large lunch and later an equally heavy supper. She was very careful, though, about *what* she ate. She ate little meat but large quantities of eggs, fruit, and vegetables. She drank volumes of coffee and tea. Extremely tidy in dress and housekeeping, Fanny was especially fussy about her wig, which had to be "just so" before she would come downstairs, according to her grandniece, Florence Paine. Every morning she had someone read one of the New York papers to her.

During her free moments at home, Fanny spent a great deal of time at the piano in the Booth parlor. According to Mrs. Paine, she "could go from one extreme to another," beginning with a classical composition, proceeding to her own hymns, finishing with ragtime. She delighted in "pepping things up"—playing old hymns in a jazzed-up style. She also improvised and invented compositions of her own but would not permit anyone to write them down. She enjoyed singing; New York friends reported that at their sing-alongs she would cry out, "Open the window and let this music rise to heaven!"

Nearly every day at home, she was met by a solid stream of visitors on pilgrimage, as it were, to see the saint of Wells Street. So many wanted to meet her that they had to call Eva Cleaveland for appointments. People came from all walks of life, for all sorts of reasons. Many asked her advice in educating or rehabilitating a blind child, and this was especially hard for her.

People sought her help writing poetry, and she never withheld assistance. Some came who had no talent at all, but Fanny did get the opportunity to coach people with real ability. One was a young neighbor girl, Blanche Simpson, who came once a week. The poet was highly impressed with the girl's verse and did all she could to assist in developing her talents. After each session, she assigned Blanche a poem to write in a particular meter or style. She also counseled Blanche about business matters, telling her there were publishing companies (not necessarily Biglow and Main) that did take advantage of those who provided them with hymns. She confided to Blanche that at times she had been taken advantage of by certain persons and cautioned her to beware.

Many came for her autograph; to accommodate them, she learned to write her name. Unscrupulous people also called on Aunt Fanny. Some seized articles of her clothing or jewelry and kept them as relics.

People appealed to Fanny by mail, too. An invalid woman in Missouri wrote for money to buy medicine. Others wrote for assistance in publishing poetry.

Fanny's day usually ended at midnight. During the evenings, she dictated replies to correspondence and then retired to her room, where she prayed and wrote hymns for several hours. In later years, she slept poorly and spent hours awake in prayer for the intentions of those who had besought her by day. She also prayed for churches and other Christian institutions. By dawn, she was usually asleep.

The one fact most people knew about Fanny Crosby was that she was blind. Far from feeling self-pity, Fanny felt that on the whole, blindness was a special gift of God. She often said, "It was the best thing that could have happened to me," and "How in the world could I have lived such a helpful life as I have lived had I not been blind?" She felt she would never have had the opportunity for an education had she not been blind. Had she not gone to

> FANNY FELT THAT ON THE WHOLE, BLINDNESS WAS A SPECIAL GIFT OF GOD.

the Institution in New York, she would not have had the contacts to enable her to write hymns for a nationally known publishing firm.

Moreover, she believed that sight must be a distraction. She attributed her great powers of concentration to blindness. She also felt that her lack of sight enabled her to develop a wonderful memory and enhanced her appeal as a speaker, creating a bond of sympathy between her and her audiences that made them more receptive to the Gospel message.

Fanny had very acute hearing and was sensitive to any discordance or disharmony. Once a man who had been denied access to visit her because she was asleep got her to wake and come out of her hotel room simply by walking down the hall and whistling off-key.

Many wondered whether she harbored some bitterness toward the fraudulent doctor who prescribed the poultices that burned her eyes. She would always say tenderly, *"Don't* blame the doctor. He is probably dead before this time. But if I could meet him, I would tell him that he unwittingly did me the greatest favor in the world." Besides, she often expressed doubt whether even the best medical treatment could have helped her already defective eyes.

Fanny felt her lack of sight was more than compensated for by a "soul-vision" that she felt was made keener by physical darkness. She believed she could see into the spiritual world. Apparently, she was often aware of the state of the souls of persons with whom she dealt. She could tell who was sincere, who was phony, who was malevolent, and who was good-hearted.

Fanny's spiritual counsel was so helpful and uplifting that many people asked her to write about her theology, but "I have never thought much about theology," she would say. She had no interest in theology in the sense of an academic discipline in which religious beliefs are systematized or put on a philosophic basis. She saw spiritual

SHE NEVER ASKED HERSELF, "IS THIS RATIONAL?" OR "IS THIS LOGICAL?" SHE ASKED, "IS THIS FROM GOD?"

wisdom proceeding not so much from the mind as from the heart and soul and from fellowship with Christ. She never asked herself, "Is this rational?" or "Is this logical?" She asked, "Is this from God?"

These convictions let her transcend the bounds of denominationalism. To her, people were "brothers" or "sisters" no matter what church they belonged to, if they believed in Jesus Christ as revealed by scripture.

The ultimate authority in Fanny Crosby's life of faith was the Bible. She lived into the time when biblical critics were taking scripture apart and seemingly reassembling it according to the inclinations of human reason. Fanny was disturbed by this phenomenon, believing the Bible to be the "absolute authority" for the Christian life. Reason should be employed to help understand scripture, but scripture should not be subordinated to what its interpreters feel is "rational." For Fanny, scripture was the absolute "norm of faith."

In her later years, Fanny was often asked where she stood regarding the Bible. Such questions vexed her sorely. "I have no time to cavil over the Sacred Volume or raise questions of no value about the Word," she said.

She felt a sermon should be preached and received as an oracle from heaven, and clergymen in their messages should be absolutely faithful to sacred scripture. For a pastor to preach on politics or poetry was a heresy that has "done more real harm to the growth of the kingdom of God among men than anything else."

For Fanny, the true essence of Christianity was something to which the scriptures and sacraments merely pointed: a real and personal relationship with God. Fanny went to God with all her needs, great and small, firmly believing God answered prayers—if the request were in the best interest of the one who prayed.

Fanny was not of the school that thinks there is no evil in life. She believed in a real Satan and believed the evil in the world is real. And although He does not "order" it, God permits evil at times in order to bring good from it. As an example of this, Fanny cited the case of her own blindness.

She could be incredibly cheerful, even in suffering. She knew there *was* always a good reason for affliction. She would often quote Hebrews 12:6, saying, "Whom the Lord loveth, He chasteneth," and commenting, "If I had no troubles, I'd think the Lord didn't love me!"

Many supposed the cheerful disposition that manifested itself in Fanny's later years was the result of a naturally happy disposition, but this was not necessarily so. We have seen how she was much beset by depression and discouragement early in life, and even in old age she admitted that her "life has been short of many things that some people would probably die rather than be without." She had suffered, but in later years she could look back and see how God had brought her through.

Often asked why some of her happiest hymns were death hymns, Fanny replied, "Since my childhood, death has simply seemed to me a stepping-stone to something better. Why should I be sad about that? I have had moments when it almost seemed I had reached heaven. Could I possibly be less happy when I reach home for good?"

Of her dead relatives, she was often heard to say, "Oh, well, they're better off. They've just passed into the glorious land." In that glorious

> "SINCE MY CHILDHOOD, DEATH HAS SIMPLY SEEMED TO ME A STEPPING-STONE TO SOMETHING BETTER."

land she expected to see them again. Of her destination, she was so certain that she criticized Lord Tennyson for writing, "I hope to see my Pilot face to face when I have crossed the bar." Fanny's correction: "I *know* I'll meet my Pilot face to face!"

Her joy was not merely a calm and "holy" serenity, a dignified and subdued felicity, but often an outright jollity. She was considered a very funny person. A great practical jokester as a girl, she was mischievous even in old age. Her sermons and lectures were full of funny stories. She felt the best way to chide or criticize was by making people laugh at their own foibles.

Indeed, she often showed disapproval through a humorous comment. Once, at Phoebe Knapp's apartments, she met a grave, pompous bishop and was turned off by his overdone sobriety. When the churchman had to excuse himself to leave, Fanny called out loudly, in the presence of the other guests, "For heaven's sake, Bishop, stay sober!"

But she disliked talk that made light of sacred things. Once, after an insolent young caller had left, she remarked to Florence, "Oh, for a hammer to knock a lump of reverence into that man's head!"

Aunt Fanny always had a special love for children. Whenever she spoke in a church, she would usually give a "children's sermon" in addition to the regular talk. She loved to play with her grandnieces and nephews and the neighborhood children. At times, when she was in town, parents would leave their little ones in Aunt Fanny's care.

By the time she was in her early eighties, Fanny was known as "the Methodist saint." Social worker Ann Cobham, whom Fanny frequently visited at her Pennsylvania estate, was not alone when she said the hymnist was "the most wonderful person living."

23
THE SAD SUMMER

"I am staying indoors until the weather shall moderate," Fanny wrote to White during the winter of 1907–1908. She seldom went out now in wintertime, but she was far from idle, with streams of visitors who came for advice and help. When the weather improved, away she went. In March, she boarded the train at Bridgeport and traveled alone to New York, where she was met by Phoebe, with whom she spent a week.

At her annual banquet, she was asked about her more than eight thousand hymns. Which did she consider the best? Significantly, she remarked, "I have not yet written my best hymn."

> **"I HAVE NOT YET WRITTEN MY BEST HYMN."**

Although she felt many of her hymns had been used by God for great good, she still felt that from an artistic point of view she had not written many great ones. Her output had been rushed. Perhaps now, since much less was being asked of her, she could get down to writing her greatest.

After her birthday, Fanny spent a week at a Methodist convention in Brooklyn. One afternoon she called on Ira Sankey in what would be her last visit to this beloved old friend. Ira was dying. For three years he had suffered from a sickness that caused him severe pain and reduced him to a near skeleton. When Fanny told him "the entire Christian world is praying for your recovery," he shook his head. He bade Fanny to meet him in heaven, "at the pearly gate at the eastern side of the city." There, he said, "I'll take you by the hand and lead you along the golden street, up to the throne of God, and there we'll stand. . .and say to Him: 'And now we see Thee face to face, saved by Thy matchless, boundless grace!' "

After the convention, Fanny set off for Perth Amboy, New Jersey, for two weeks of speaking engagements. Although she must have known she was seeing Sankey for the last time, when she bade adieu to Phoebe Knapp at the Hotel Savoy, she had no way of knowing that for her, too, it was to be the last good-bye.

From there she proceeded to Princeton, where she spoke at a "sacred concert" on Good Friday at the Presbyterian church. On Sunday, she preached the Easter sermon.

Before leaving Princeton, she paid one last visit to her old friend, Grover Cleveland, who was feeble and emaciated. She was deeply concerned about him as she rode to New Haven, where she visited Bert White at Yale. On the morning of June 25, she learned Grover was dead. She consoled herself that they had had a "deep, warm friendship that death cannot break, for the cords will be united and we shall see and know each other in the land of the blest."

It was to be the saddest summer of Fanny's long life. Little more than two weeks after she learned of Cleveland's death, she was stunned by the news that Phoebe had died. Still vigorous and youthful-looking in her early seventies, Phoebe had gone to Poland Spring, Maine, for a vacation and there, on July 10, had suffered a stroke.

A month later, Sankey's soul was freed. He drifted off into a coma on the morning of August 13, singing the opening lines of Fanny's "Saved by Grace":

Some day the silver cord will break
And I no more as now shall sing,
But, oh, the joy when I shall wake
Within the palace of the King!

By nightfall, he was gone.

Fanny must have felt quite lonely. Not only had she outlived most of her friends her own age; she had outlived most of those who were a generation younger. Unlike many very old persons who wonder why they are left behind, Fanny remained basically "as happy as a chickadee," secure in the confidence that she eventually would be united forever with those she had loved and secure in the confidence that God still had work for her to do on earth.

She continued to write hymns, mostly for Allan Sankey and Charles Gabriel, a few for Hugh Main. For Main, she wrote a successful hymn on the transitory nature of earthly life titled "We're Traveling On." It was the last of her major hymns.

She continued to speak regularly at the Christian Union and maintained her ministry of cheer by private meetings, letters, lectures, and hospital visitations.

Fanny's lifetime had spanned many changes in America. She had seen the invention of the telephone, telegraph, steam engine, phonograph, moving picture, bicycle, typewriter, X-ray, elevator, sewing machine, safety match, anesthetics, reaper and mower, submarine, typesetting machine, automobile, airplane, and radio. She came to know and somewhat appreciate modern poetry—poetry without rhyme and rhythm, so unlike that which she wrote. She enjoyed the popular songs of the day and toyed with the idea of writing secular songs once again, as she had done fifty years before. She felt her lyrics could "elevate above their present standard" the songs of the day.

Aunt Fanny was profoundly disturbed by other trends she saw developing in American society: the growing tendency toward materialism and the beginning of the breakdown of the American home and family structure. At odds with the feminist movement, she complained that modern women seemed eager to do everything but "the work that ought to be done at home." She added, "I may appear a little old-fogeyish, but I have firm convictions on this very vital question." She was convinced the strength of a nation lay in family and home life; when that broke down, so did the nation.

At the center of the home should be God, and Fanny saw with great concern the decreasing interest in Christianity among Americans. "When I was a child," she said of the Bible, "this book had a practical place both in home and nation." The growing doubts and disbelief of scripture saddened her. "No Christian nation can be great which ignores the Sacred Book," she lamented. And America could not endure "if the heads of the families are prayerless."

> FANNY SAW WITH GREAT CONCERN THE DECREASING INTEREST IN CHRISTIANITY AMONG AMERICANS.

She felt the nation, too, must be headed by a man of prayer. William H. Taft, a rather nominal Unitarian, was in the White House. Fanny said she felt it was impossible for the nation to survive with "prayerless presidents." Without a return to the faith of their fathers, America had no future at all.

She saw all this reflected in the life of the church itself, where attendance was falling off. She was appalled at the small number of men interested in religion. She feared that from the generation rising about her "there will not be men enough in heaven to sing bass."

Within Protestantism were movements that appalled Fanny.

Many modern theologians had come to question the authority of scripture. Fanny was deeply troubled about trends she perceived developing among the clergy. She was troubled when told of many young people losing their faith in college and seminary.

Fanny seldom went to church services now. The infrequency of her attendance is a mystery. She was growing quite frail, but this did not stop her from traveling up and down the East Coast to speak. About the only times she appeared at First Methodist Church now were when she was asked to speak. When asked by friends about her infrequent attendance, she said, "I can worship God just as well here, by myself, as I can at church." This is a baffling statement, coming from a lifelong churchgoer.

Fanny retained her Methodist membership, however, and continued to work diligently with the King's Daughters. She became increasingly interested in Roman Catholicism, finding it a "good, strong religion" whose fervent piety she admired. She held in highest respect Pius X, who had opposed the trends toward "modernism" among his own clergy and people and who was noted for the extraordinary holiness of his life. The only drawback she saw with the Roman Catholic faith was not doctrinal but liturgical.

Not all the developments within Protestantism filled her with dismay. She followed with interest the career of Dr. W. A. (Billy) Sunday, who in many ways proved himself a successor to her dear Moody. She also was inspired by Dr. J. Wilbur Chapman and his "chorister" Charles M. (Charlie) Alexander,

SHE FOLLOWED WITH INTEREST THE CAREER OF BILLY SUNDAY.

who in 1909 conducted a successful multinational campaign. She even wrote a poem in their honor.

In March 1910, Fanny celebrated her ninetieth birthday. She

was bent nearly double but continued to travel and lecture, refusing to give in to the ravages of time. She wrote Bert White that "I am so busy I hardly know my name." Her cheerfulness seemed to increase rather than diminish. She maintained that "I don't want to die yet, but rather live on for another decade-and-a-half, to the age of a hundred and five." Yet if her heavenly Father willed otherwise, she conceded, "it is well." She attributed her longevity to "angel-guards" who controlled her appetite, temper, and speech.

Fanny traveled to New York alone in the spring of 1911, where she appeared as the principal speaker at the "Tent, Open-Air and Shop Campaign" of the Evangelistic Committee of the Methodist Episcopal Church. More than five thousand people were at Carnegie Hall that day, and a choir of two thousand sang, almost exclusively, her hymns.

Fanny arrived in an automobile. When it pulled up, the attendants were so appalled by her ravaged appearance that one of them cried, "For heaven's sake, get a wheelchair!"

Fanny's strong voice stopped them. "I need no rolling chair. I can stand on my own two feet. My strength is in the Lord."

That October, she returned to New York for the last time to visit Helen Keller, whom she had met a decade before. After a day with her gifted friend, whom she considered a modern prophet, Fanny once more visited the Bowery Mission and spoke there. Then she went to Jersey City, where she spoke at the Simpson Memorial Methodist Church and visited Alice Holmes, who at ninety was somewhat deaf and feeble. The two women had not been together for four decades, but Alice recognized Fanny at once by her voice.

That autumn, everyone felt the last hour had come for Aunt Fanny when she was stricken with pneumonia, but to everyone's amazement—including her own—she recovered. She looked so frail now that everyone expected her death momentarily.

But she still traveled occasionally. In February 1913, she and Florence journeyed to Cambridge, Massachusetts, to speak at the First Baptist Church. At one service she preached to an audience of two thousand. Years later, a man who had been a child at the time remembered "the little old lady, dressed in black, standing with Dr. Campbell behind the lectern, saying good-bye to the world."

Her ninety-third birthday fell on Easter, and she remarked, "If there is anyone in this world happier than I, I want to shake his hand, for I believe myself to be as happy as it is possible for a mortal to be in this world. Life with me glides on like a little boat on a waveless stream, with flowers on each bank."

That evening she appeared at the First Methodist Church for the first time in many months. George Stebbins had come from Brooklyn to be with her, accompanied by his neighbor Mrs. Jenny Bennett Carpenter, a blind soprano. Fanny had heard her sing while on a visit to New York several years earlier and had been impressed by her talent. After Fanny spoke and blessed the congregation, Mrs. Carpenter sang "Saved by Grace." Halfway through, Aunt Fanny rose, took her arm, and sang with her. The congregation was moved to tears by the sight of the two blind women singing together.

Fanny spent her time now, as she said in a letter to Bert White, "knitting, always as usual—stopping when callers come in or something more pressing presents itself." She took a few automobile rides and a few trips to see friends, but beyond that she seldom went out anymore. As her ninety-fourth birthday approached, the King's Daughters decided all Fanny's friends should honor her by wearing her favorite flower, the violet. Hugh Main saw to it that Violet Day came to the attention of the newspapers, and another nationwide birthday celebration was planned.

The Sunday before Violet Day, Fanny spoke for what was to be the last time—at First Methodist. The church was packed. A local newspaper reported Fanny was "feeble in body, yet strong in mind. . .buoyant in spirit, with a trust and faith in God as firm as the everlasting hills."

Most of her address was about the power of prayer. Prayer is essential in the life of the believer, she said. Some people think one must kneel or assume a certain position to pray, but this, she said, is false. "I do not kneel to pray. I no longer have the strength to rise from that position." Believers should feel free to pray wherever or in whatever position is most convenient.

> **MOST OF HER ADDRESS WAS ABOUT THE POWER OF PRAYER.**

She gave several examples of God answering prayers, including her own recovery from pneumonia, which she attributed solely to the prayers of her friends. "I want all of you to go to God in prayer in all trials and sorrows. The good will come out of it, and He will answer your prayer better than you think." Of course, one may not always get exactly what is requested, she said. But one must trust God's way as best.

She urged the congregation to "cling to the Saviour" in "this age of change." She concluded, "My dear, dear people, I love you dearly, and if I should first cross to the beautiful shore, I know that I shall greet you there!" But she felt her work was not yet done. "I believe that He still has work for me yet. I don't want to die yet."

But it was now apparent to most and probably to her that she would not approximate her goal of 105 years.

24
THE MORN OF ZION'S GLORY

The last day of May, Fanny and Jule celebrated their mother's birthday once more at Jule's home. Approaching death was very much in the minds of the two old women, and Fanny repeatedly said of Carrie, "I know that she is very near me." She also claimed "communion of the spirit" with Ira Sankey and said it would be a grand day when she went to heaven to once more "behold the sweet faces" of those she had loved.

In August 1914, Fanny suffered a mild heart attack. She again believed her time had come. During the illness, she had ecstatic visions, and when she was better, she reported that these were the most remarkable of her life. She said very little about their nature, except that in one an angel came to her and said, "Be thou faithful, and I will give thee the crown of life"—an almost word-for-word quotation from the Apocalypse of John. The angel also said, "Be calm and get your strength back as soon as you can, and then go to work for the Master once more."

Fanny partially recovered, but the doctors told Florence her aunt could not live many more months. Fanny welcomed her approaching end with joy. She was going to "just pass on to the glorious land," and she told her friends, "When I have arrived at my

FANNY WELCOMED HER APPROACHING END WITH JOY.

eternal home, they will say, 'Come in, Fanny! Come in!' Then will be the victory through Christ!"

But as the angel had bidden, while life lasted, she still had "work for the Master." First and foremost, Fanny felt that the angel wanted her to give the world a few more hymns before she departed. Indeed, Allan Sankey and Hugh Main were planning their first major hymnal in a decade and asked Fanny to contribute. In the next few months, she wrote about a dozen hymns. Among the best was "Keep Thou Me."

In January, the aged Doane, suffering from "creeping paralysis" and bedridden, able to sit up for only a few minutes each day, decided to write one last song. He sent word to his old colleague that he would like her to write the lyrics. In early February, she wrote what was to prove her hymnic swan song:

At evening time it shall be light,
When fades the day of toil away,
No shadows deep, no weary night,
At evening time, it shall be light.

At evening time it shall be light,
Immortal love from realms above
Is breathing now the promise bright,
At evening time it shall be light.

Fanny began to make preparations for her death and burial. She made Florence and Jule promise any memorial in her memory would not be a marble or granite monument, such as Barnum had erected to himself close to her plot, but something that could benefit people. She had several suggestions. The Christian Union had been a concern ever since she had come to Bridgeport, and it needed an infirmary. If her friends felt they had to memorialize her, let them set up a fund in her name to raise money for this.

Or perhaps her friends could found a home for elderly people. Although her own life had been made cheerful by a young family and young friends, she was concerned with the loneliness and emptiness in the lives of so many older people in a society in which the increasing tendency was for children to live apart from their aging parents and grandparents. One elderly widow told her the only time she ever heard a human voice was when the woman she hired to keep house summoned her to a meal. Fanny thought it might be a good thing if elderly people who had no families could live together in a community; this might be a suitable memorial for her.

Or perhaps it could take the form of a fund to help elderly ministers, for whom there was no real pension system in those days. But by no means was any money to be spent on a tombstone or dead marble monument.

Fanny called in a lawyer to draw up a will in which she left half of her estate to Florence, in gratitude for accommodating her for so many years. The other half was to be held in trust by Florence for Jule, an arrangement Fanny decided on because of her sister's advancing years. When Jule should die, her share would go to Florence.

On February 8, Fanny was visited by a group of mission workers, and she spoke of her life, telling them she was especially concerned with four categories of people: railroad men, policemen, prisoners, and the poor. To the mission workers, Fanny reiterated what she had said all her life about her blindness: "The loss of sight has been no loss to me."

During her last weeks, Fanny manifested a peculiar phenomenon. Numerous visitors remarked with wonder that her countenance seemed visibly to shine "full of radiant light." The visible glowing first was observed on isolated occasions as early as 1907, but apparently it became constant in her last days. It was noted by the mission workers and by Rev. H. A. Davenport of the People's Presbyterian Church, who called on her February 9.

On the tenth, Adam Geibel came, and the two blind musicians played a duet at the piano. On the eleventh, Fanny said she did not feel well and would stay in bed. Her appetite, always so good, had failed. "Tomorrow I shall be well," she said, and she seemed radiant with joy. All through the day she smiled and kept saying, "I'm so comfortable. I'm so comfortable."

At nine that night, she sent for Eva Cleaveland and asked her to take down a letter to a neighbor family who had just lost a child, assuring them "your precious Ruth is 'Safe in the Arms of Jesus.'" After completing the letter, she dictated her final testimony to the world:

> *In the morn of Zion's glory,*
> *When the clouds have rolled away,*
> *And my hope has dropped its anchor*
> *In the vale of perfect day,*
> *When with all the pure and holy*
> *I shall strike my harp anew,*
> *With a power no arm can sever,*
> *Love will hold me fast and true.*

Henry Booth was the last one in the household to retire that night. When he came upstairs at two thirty in the morning, he looked in, as he always did, to see how Aunt Fanny was. She was awake, heard him, smiled, and said gently, "All right, Governor." At three thirty, Florence heard her aunt walking down the hall. Getting up to assist her, she met Fanny at the doorway to her room. There, to her horror, Fanny fainted in her arms.

Florence carried the meager figure back to bed, awoke her

husband and son, and called two doctors. Fanny was oblivious to those around the bedside. Earth seemed to be receding now, "the morn of Zion's glory" breaking upon her. Florence and Henry were struck by the peace and serenity on her face.

The first of the doctors arrived about four thirty and pronounced her dead of a massive cerebral hemorrhage. Florence screamed and burst into tears, sobbing, "It cannot be! It cannot be!" Eva Cleaveland, however, confided in a letter to Bert White, "We have had reason to fear that she might have a long unconscious illness or suffer or something that way, so that it is a comfort to have her go like this."

According to many witnesses, Fanny Crosby's was the largest funeral ever seen in Bridgeport, surpassing even that of P. T. Barnum. People stood for blocks to file by the bier. At her right hand was the little silk flag she had always carried. On the casket, at the request of Jule, were engraved the words, *My Sister*.

George Stebbins, Allan Sankey, and Hugh Main were there. The church was full of the flowers Fanny had loved. The choir sang her favorite hymn, Heber's "Faith of Our Fathers." Pastor Davenport prayed at great length. Then the choir sang "Safe in the Arms of Jesus" and "Saved by Grace" as many wept openly.

Dr. Brown, in his eulogy, said, "You have come to pay tribute and to crown a friend. There must have been a royal welcome when this queen of sacred song burst the bonds of death and passed into the glories of heaven."

Poetic tributes were read. As the congregation filed out, everyone was given a violet. Passing before the bier, they dropped the flowers in until it seemed she was sleeping in a bed of violets.

The rest of Fanny's associates began to die. On Christmas Eve, Doane succumbed to pneumonia at eighty-four. Three days later, Allan Sankey had a heart attack—a week after his marriage to the widow Anna Underhill Neighams. Eliza Hewitt, after major surgery, died in April 1920. The next year, Kirkpatrick died of a heart attack while writing a hymn. Hugh Main retired; his firm was merged with the Hope Publishing Company of Chicago; he died at eighty-six in October 1925.

George Stebbins lived on in Catskill, New York, continuing to write music and giving a setting to at least one previously unused poem of Fanny's. He died in October 1945, four months short of his one-hundredth birthday.

Of Fanny's family, Jule died of cancer at eighty in January 1921; she was Fanny's last close blood relation. Florence Booth died in 1935, her husband, Henry, in 1946. Adelbert White, after a distinguished career at the University of Nebraska, died in 1951. Eva Cleaveland, her faithful secretary, lived in Bridgeport until 1956.

In 1920, on the one-hundredth anniversary of Fanny's birth, an infirmary was opened by the Christian Union in memory of its benefactress. Two years later, a twenty-eight-room mansion was endowed in Bridgeport as the Fanny Crosby Memorial Home for aged men and women.

Until 1955, there was nothing to mark Fanny Crosby's grave except a tiny marble stone with the words *Aunt Fanny* and the inscription, "She hath done what she could." Even that was more than she had asked. But on May 1 that year, a large marble slab was erected on her grave because Bridgeport citizens decided the "relatively inconspicuous marker with only vague identification" was unworthy.

The new inscription concludes with a verse from her famous hymn:

Blessed assurance, Jesus is mine!
Oh, what a foretaste of glory divine!
Heir of salvation, purchase of God,
Born of His spirit, washed in His blood.